The English
Vicarage Garden

The title page illustration shows Rosa 'Jacob's Coat' at St. Mary's Portsea.

The English Vicarage Garden

Thirty gardens of beauty and inspiration

Introduced by
Miss Read

Text by
Piers Dudgeon

A Mermaid Book

MICHAEL JOSEPH LTD · PILOT PRODUCTIONS LTD

Published by the Penguin Group
27 Wrights Lane, London, W8 5TZ, England

In association with Pilot Productions Ltd
17 Munster Road, London, SW6 4ER

Viking Penguin Inc., 40 West 23rd Street, New York, New York 10010, USA
Penguin Books Australia Ltd, Ringwood, Victoria, Australia
Penguin Books Canada Ltd, 2801 John Street, Markham, Ontario, Canada L3R 1B4
Penguin Books (NZ) Ltd, 182-190 Wairau Road, Auckland 10, New Zealand

Penguin Books Ltd. Registered Offices, Harmondsworth, Middlesex, England

First published May 1988
First published in Mermaid Books March 1991
Copyright © Pilot Productions Limited 1988
Introduction Copyright © Miss Read 1988

Edited by Piers Dudgeon
Designed by Mike Ricketts
Typeset by Dorchester Typesetting, Dorset, England
Printed by Mandarin, Hong Kong

A CIP catalogue record for this book is
available from the British Library
ISBN hardback 0 7181 2911 3
      paperback 0 7181 3363 3

Acknowledgements

Pilot Productions would like to thank everyone who has helped in the production of this book, not least the Bishops, Archdeacons, Rectors and Vicars of the Church of England, and their wives, who imparted information and so generously gave of their time, hospitality and thoughts. Some seventy gardens were visited (and many more recommended) but because of strict limits of space, sadly there have had to be omissions.

Quotations from 'The Crest on the Silver' by Geoffrey Grigson, The Cresset Press, 1950, and from 'An Englishman's Garden' by Edward Hyams, Thames and Hudson, 1967.

Photographs by Piers Dudgeon, Nick Wright, The Revd. R. Blakeway-Phillips, 'Focus 3', Dr. June Chatfield of the Gilbert White Museum, Michael Warren, the BBC Hulton Picture Library, the Bodleian Library, Oxford (MS. Eng. misc. e.251, f.1(R)), the British Library, the National Library of Wales, the Oxford City Library, The Woodmansterne Picture Library, the Harry Smith Photographic Collection, and the Royal Botanical Gardens, Kew. Permissions also granted by the Robert Harding Picture Library, The Royal Horticultural Society and the Revd. Michael Perry.

Line illustrations by Vana Haggerty.

Our thanks, too, to Ms. Ann Bonar for her advice and checking of plant nomenclature, Mrs. John Hole, the Hon. Mrs. H.E. Boscawen, Mrs. Sarah Beer and Mrs. Lilian Thornhill for their information and photographs relating to Dean Hole, Canon A.T. Boscawen, Canon Charles Kingsley and the Revd. William Wilks, respectively.

Contents

St. Mary's, Portsea, where over 200 different roses are grown.
'He who would have beautiful roses in his garden must have beautiful roses in his heart,'
wrote the rosarian, Dean Samuel Reynolds Hole, in 1869.

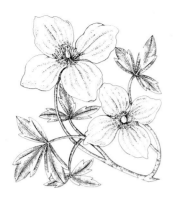

Introduction

MISS READ

I suppose that the phrase 'English vicarage garden' evokes for most of us a vision of striped lawns, herbaceous borders and ancient cedar trees, all bathed in the gentle sunshine of a summer's afternoon.

It is understandable. When I was young, most vicarage gardens had a gardener to augment the incumbent's efforts, and church gardens were well-kept even when the vicar was not himself a gardener. The general public, whether churchgoers or not, were invited into these pleasances on specified summer afternoons to enjoy all the fun of the fair, bowling for the pig, riding on a miniature railway, home-made teas in a tent, and innumerable stalls, to raise funds for the church roof, the organ, or any other of those ecclesiastical casualties which, like the poor, are always with us.

Even if you balked at the energy-consuming attractions, it was very pleasant to wander round the less populated parts of the vicar's garden, comparing the progress of his runner beans with your own, noting the condition of his compost heap and the way the laurels, planted by a long-dead predecessor were completely out of hand.

I am sure that I must have visited a number of vicarage gardens in my early years, for my parents were churchgoers, and my maiden aunts were stalwart helpers in Sunday schools, church bazaars and fêtes. My bachelor Uncle Harry was also active in such affairs through his support of the YMCA. But the vicarage garden I remember most clearly was one in Kent when I was about eight or nine. A fund-raising fête was held in dazzling sunshine. Everything proper to the occasion was there; the cake stall, the coconut shies, the bustling tea-ladies. And best of all, the penny stall, where I bought a magnificent white ostrich-feather fan which was heavily moult-ing, but no less enchanting. Perhaps, for me, that Edwardian relic accounts for the happiness I feel when the subject of vicarage gardens crops up, that vision of a blessed plot where it is always summer afternoon.

But that vision seems to be widely shared. Is it simply because so many summer functions were held here, in the local out-of-doors parish room? Or is it because the English vicarage garden embodies a wider vision of England's 'green and pleasant land'? Certainly no one has evoked the atmosphere better than Rupert Brooke, who wrote longingly of his home at the Old Vicarage, Grantchester, as he lay ill in Berlin in 1912:

'Just now the lilac is in bloom
All before my little room;
And in my flower-beds, I think
Smile the carnation and the pink;
And down the borders, well I know,
The poppy and the pansy blow . . .'

Somehow, clergymen and their gardens go together in the layman's view, probably because in days gone by the garden, like the church and the vicarage itself, exerted a strong influence on the pattern of a clergyman's life. Many writers have made us poignantly aware of the special quality of the life of a rural English vicar. In 'Summoned By Bells' John Betjeman writes of a Cornish rector, earlier this century:

'I found St. Ervan's partly ruined church.
Its bearded Rector, holding in one hand
A gong-stick, in the other hand a book,
Struck, while he read, a heavy-sounding bell,
Hung from an elm bough by the churchyard gate.

The main lawn of the Old Vicarage, Grantchester, where 'oft between the boughs is seen/The sly shade of a Rural Dean.' Rupert Brooke

"Better come in. It's time for Evensong."
There wasn't much to see, there wasn't much
The Little Guide *could say about the church.*
Holy and small and heavily restored,
It held me for the length of Evensong,
Said rapidly among discoloured walls,
Impatient of my diffident response.
"Better come in and have a cup of tea,"
The Rectory was large, uncarpeted;
Books and oil-lamps and papers were about;
The study's pale green walls were mapped with damp;
The pitch-pine doors and window-frames were cracked;
Loose noisy tiles along the passages
Led to a waste of barely furnished rooms:
Clearly the rector lived here all alone.
He talked of poetry and Cornish saints;
He kept an apiary and a cow . . .'

That rural loneliness, that mixture of poetry, piety and apiary, can still be found, and may be one of the reasons for the affection felt by many incumbents for their gardens, as much a comfort to them as it is to their parishioners. But perhaps the eighteenth-century clergyman-diarists most surely and sharply conveyed the atmosphere of clerical life and the close connection between parson and garden.

The first of the great clergyman-diarists who springs to mind is Gilbert White, who wrote so lovingly of his garden at Selborne. Strangely enough, he was never the Vicar of Selborne, although he was born in the vicarage, but he was Curate of Selborne on four occasions.

His garden at The Wakes, as his house was called, was originally quite small, but in 1760 he acquired an adjoining plot of land which gave him much more scope.

It was not only the plants and trees which he observed so minutely and wrote about so meticulously, but the animals and birds he encountered there.

'A moist and warm afternoon, with the thermometer at 50, brought forth troops of shell-snails; and at the same juncture, the tortoise heaved up the mould

The vicarage garden at Torpenhow in Cumbria, the thirteenth-century home of the Reverend David Scott, for whom the garden is literally an inspiration. His book, 'A Quiet Gathering', won the prestigious Geoffrey Faber Memorial prize for poetry.

and put out its head; and the next morning came forth, as it were raised from the dead; and walked about until four in the afternoon.'

And again:

'The *white owl* does indeed snore and hiss in a tremendous manner; and these menaces well answer the intention of intimidating; for I have known a whole village up in arms on such an occasion, imagining the churchyard to be full of goblins and spectres.'

At much the same time another clerical diarist was writing at Weston Longville near Norwich.

The Reverend James Woodford kept his diary from 1758 until his death in 1802, but the major part of it was written in his Norfolk parish which he cared for from 1776 until his end. He too was an apiarist, and took great interest in his bees noting that one of his swarms had to be hived twice as the first hive was rejected. 'It had been kept in the Corn Chamber, and perhaps Mice might have been in it. Bees are particularly Nice and Cleanly,' he wrote.

His love of food produces many glimpses of the vegetables and fruit grown in the vicarage garden. A fine dish of early peas, a 'gooseberry pye', peaches from the wall. And sometimes Mr. Custance ('My Squire') is 'exceedingly kind' and calls with 'a very fine melon.'

In January 1782 he writes: 'Busy all the morning in my garden, having enlarged my Pleasure Ground.' On June 2nd, four years later, he notes that he had this garden mown for the second time that season.

There seems to have been at least two gardeners to help Parson Woodford, but he too was active, painting the coach house doors, cleaning out his pond and helping to erect his newly-painted weather-cock. 'The Pole painted a dark-green, and the Weather-cock, black and gold. It is put in the middle of the first Clump of Firs by the front Door of the House.'

In the nineteenth century the vicarage garden began to have a wider significance. A number of clergymen gardeners began to exert an important influence on the development of the English garden as we know it today, a style of gardening wilder and more natural than before, with far more emphasis on flowers.

No doubt this was all part of the general excitement engendered by the Romantic Revival when poets such as Wordsworth and Coleridge turned to nature and made their readers aware of the joys to be found in plants and flowers as well as 'the rocks and

Part of the vegetable garden at the Vicarage, Childswickham, which dates back over 600 years.

stones and trees'. Later, the Pre-Raphaelite movement strengthened this feeling.

The earlier formal gardens were now out of fashion. On the grand scale Capability Brown had demonstrated the natural look. Now, smaller gardens echoed a feeling for flowing lines and made use of colour and form provided by the many new flowering plants which were arriving in this country.

For this was the age of the great Georgian and Victorian plant hunters. Joseph Banks, who sailed with Captain Cook across the world, brought back some of our best-loved plants. Many more botanists scoured the then world-wide British Empire to return with hundreds of flowering plants which we now accept as typically English.

And it was clergymen like the Boscawens of Cornwall, the Ellacombes of Gloucestershire (in each case, father and son), and Samuel Reynolds Hole of Caunton in Nottinghamshire, who were active in effecting this change. These men imported plants from abroad and created gardens of world renown in their rural rectories and vicarages. They spread the word in books and gardening articles, and cultivated new varieties of flowers.

For this was the hey-day, too, of the great plant breeders, clergymen like the Revd. Henry Harpur Crewe whose name lives on in the *Crocus crewei*, and

the double yellow wallflower, *Cheiranthus* 'Harpur Crewe'. In the long and distinguished list of clergyman horticulturalists, the name of the Revd. William Wilks may not bring an instant response, but when one learns that he was the vicar of Shirley in Surrey from January 1880, and was as dedicated a gardener as he was a clergyman, then one realises that the famous Shirley poppy was one of his plant-breeding successes.

I found the account of William Wilks particularly interesting, as I am told that I was frequently pushed in my pram to the Shirley woods for picnics. This great and good man died in 1923, honoured by *The Royal Horticultural Society* for which he did so much. It would have been nice to have had my head patted by such a fine parish priest, and quite possible, for he was a lover of little children as well as flowers.

His memory is still revered in the parish, and Miss Nina Foster, the local historian, was told of a typical gesture of William Wilks who carried an armful of daffodils into a house where a coffin lay, and placed them there. 'That was the sort of care he showed.'

One of the most valuable parts of this book is the botanical knowledge displayed by so many of its

Canon Charles Kingsley and his wife, Frances, at Eversley Rectory.

and he obviously found in his garden not only a refreshment of spirit, but many sure signs of God's manifestation in natural objects, frequently expressing his belief that 'all symmetrical natural objects, aye, and perhaps all forms, colours and scents which show organisation and arrangement, are types of some spiritual truth or existence . . .'

Francis Kilvert, that lovable Victorian clergyman, in his diaries echoes this belief. The exhilaration he felt when walking about his beloved parish of Clyro in Wales or in his father's at Langley Burrell in Wiltshire, is allied to his love for nature and the Church.

On Easter morning 1876 he writes: 'I rose early and went out into the fresh brilliant morning, listening to the rising of the lark as he went up in an ecstacy of song into the blue unclouded sky, and gave in his Easter morning hymn at Heaven's Gate. Then came the echo and answer of the earth as the Easter bells rang out their joyful peals from the Church Towers all round.

It was very sweet and lovely, the bright silent sunny morning, and the lark rising and singing alone in the blue sky, and then suddenly the morning air all alive with the music of the sweet bells ring for the joy of the Resurrection.'

Nearer our own time, the writings and exquisite botanical illustrations of the Reverend W. Keble Martin comprising a life-time's labour of love in *The Concise British Flora In Colour*, introduce us to another nature-loving clergyman. Yet again we are conscious of the reverence and delight felt in living things, and of their affinity with a greater power. 'This interest,'

A fête in the garden at the Rectory at Barton-le-Clay, Bedfordshire, which is also open to the public through the National Gardens Scheme.

contributors. To accompany a dedicated enthusiast around his garden is always educational, and to listen to his practical advice as well as his introduction to little-known species. Doubly interesting then it is to have this down in black and white, the personal account of set-backs and victories, of learning about the vagaries of one particular plot in all seasons. It is not only Gardening Made Easy, it is much more.

Throughout its pages one becomes sharply aware of the deeper meaning to these clergymen of their ministrations. The care of their gardens is an extension of their pastoral work. The teachings of the Church, its comfort and spiritual refreshment is here made manifest. The vicarage garden is a place to rest, to seek peace, and to come face to face with the rhythms and shapes of nature.

Charles Kingsley felt this deeply. In 1842 he came, as a young curate, to Eversley Rectory in Hampshire, and fell in love with the garden, sending vivid descriptions and sketches of it to the lady who later became his wife. He was an exceptionally able and lovable man, as willing to learn as he was to teach,

The garden at Bitton where Canon Henry Nicholson Ellacombe, with his famous gardening father before him, accounted for nearly 100 years of stewardship.

The roll of clergymen gardeners whose names live on through their work in the area of plant breeding is long and distinguished. The Reverend Harpur Crewe produced Cheiranthus cheiri 'Harpur Crewe' in the kitchen garden at Drayton Beauchamp where he was incumbent for twenty-three years from 1860.

he writes, 'stays with us to the end of our pilgrimage.'

It is this affinity of things mystical and natural which permeates this book in the subtlest way. It is perhaps the strongest theme which comes through, and most tellingly expressed by the wife of Canon Slade of Topcliffe near Thirsk. Together they have made a garden round the modern house which replaced the old rectory in the 1960s. 'What do I find in all this?' said Mrs. Slade. 'What I personally find is an atmosphere for prayer – I find it a marvellous situation for intercession. There's nothing really creative about housework; whereas in the garden, although a certain amount is bothering about weeds and so forth, it is also a creative activity. You are creating something which is going to last.'

But perhaps the most revealing is Canon Ellacombe's account, month by month, of the work, the blooms and the joys to be found in his famous garden at Bitton, now in Avon. His book, *In A Gloucestershire Garden*, is a chronicle which conveys in every page the sense of 'a divinity that shapes our end', and makes the reader aware how

The rectory garden at Blagdon, nestling in the Mendips. The rector's father-in-law, Prebendary F. Vere Hodge, recently planted a wild, conservationist garden which can be seen at Glastonbury on the hill above the ruined abbey.

deeply his garden contributed to the richness of his spiritual life. As instructive as he is enjoyable, no reader could close the book without feeling better for the guidance of this wise and friendly counsellor.

Dean Hole, himself a great gardener, said later, that as he believed in Eden 'as thoroughly as though I had seen it .... he believed that our love of horticulture and our happiness in a garden are reminiscences of our first glorious home, and longings to reproduce it . . .'

Certainly, one cannot read the diaries and letters of garden-loving clergymen without echoing Dean Hole's beliefs.

This feeling of a tradition going back into the mists of time, is most strongly felt, of course, in the very old vicarage gardens. One such was the garden at Yatton Keynell in Wiltshire seen one drenching May afternoon with the tulips and forget-me-nots shedding bright drops.

The garden and the house were originally monastic and the beautiful pond no doubt was once the monks' stew. Earlier in this century after a wickedly

cold spell when ice was thick for weeks on the surface, the thaw was particularly welcome. Then, it was reported, as the ice melted, the corpse of an enormous carp was sighted. How old, one wonders, was this monster?

The old serpentine wall bordering the orchard of the Old Vicarage at Nuneham Courtney in Oxfordshire also evokes this feeling, reminding one of Parson Woodforde's walled garden with nectarines, pears and peaches trained against it, just as this one once had. The fact that so many people have cared for the same plot of land, shared its quirks of climate, and soil problems, suffered the same set-backs but also rejoiced in its bounty, gives a sense of continuity.

Another much-loved garden of great age was visited one day of showers and sunshine. Here at Barton-le-Clay in Bedfordshire, the rector and his mother are the gardeners. It had been rather neglected since the war years, and the first thing to be done was to cut down fifty dead elm trees.

Earlier rectors had planted the superb copper beech and other mature trees. The pond had been tamed and surrounded by water-loving plants. When I saw it, a carp was basking just below the surface in a patch of sunlight, and the rector's dog was engrossed with a shoal of tadpoles at the edge. It was

The artificial rectangular lake, 50 yds. by 6, and the bell tower on the ancient rectory at Yatton Keynell. The house stands forward in two-and-a-half acres of garden and is bounded by a twelfth-century brick wall.

a timeless scene. How many generations, one wondered, had enjoyed this very plot?

As the rector himself said: 'More often than not the garden is swarming with people. In a minute someone will come to walk round or just sit in a chair. I say to the old people, do pop in and use it – come! I'm sure that that must have been the intention of the original vicarage gardens. They are places of renewal, of refreshment.'

This truth was echoed in a recent article in the *Daily Telegraph*, by Charles Moore, Editor of *The Spectator*, who points out that to most Englishmen 'The Church of England belongs to the people of England. Not in any shallow, democratic sense of belonging, not belonging as a piece of transferable property, but belonging as the countryside or the monarchy or a mixture of the two belongs. The Church is there, and it is there for anyone who wants it, present as a building, as a tradition, as a liturgy, as represented by clergymen . . .'

It is this feeling which comes through very strongly in so many of the following articles. The parish priest wants to share his garden as well as his church. The rector of St. Mary's, Diss, spoke for all our clergymen gardeners when he said, 'Our attitude is that the house and garden is property belonging to the parish, and we're just privileged to have it most of the time. We revel in the opportunity for others to come and enjoy it.'

Such hospitality is traditional, of course. From monastic times the gardens have given sanctuary from violence or danger, and also provided medicinal herbs for natural remedies for the sick of the community. The very old vicarage gardens sometimes sprout rare and ancient herbs, just as the nearby churchyards harbour hoary old yew trees which traditionally supplied local bowmen with their bows.

It is this sense of history which the English cherish. Whether they are church-goers or not, it is to the church, the churchyard, and the vicarage garden

Looking across the ornamental lake towards the vicarage garden of St. Michael with St. Mary in Melbourne, Derbyshire.

whenever available, that they wend their way when they are having a day out. Americans cross the Atlantic, notebooks in hand, to 'find their roots'. Tombstones, parish registers, the Record Office, all help in their searches, but very often it is the rector himself, in his study or his garden, who can supply the vital clue. It is he who knows that old Mrs so-and-so treasures a diary of her grandfather's which has a bearing on this particular searcher's history, and sends his visitor, replete with vicarage tea, to a nearby cottage.

For it is still the vicar who is looked upon by most people as the chief man of the parish. Just as earlier generations went to find remedies from the herbarium, so do present-day visitors call at the vicarage for comfort. Sometimes it is a personal matter, an unhappy marriage, a financial problem, even a question of health which a doctor cannot explain. Sometimes a reference is required, a signature needed or advice sought. Over the years, the vicarage study, and often the vicarage garden, have heard confidences concerned with the full range of human perplexities. It is the *availability* of help which people cherish, the traditions of an institution which is always there.

The incumbents themselves are very conscious of this tradition, and of the fact that they are only a transient part of this continuing force. It does not matter if their house is a new one, their garden still raw, their parish largely made up of new estates peopled by newcomers, this great tradition of service, of help in time of trouble, and of instant and constant hospitality still shines through.

On St. George's Day at Blagdon one had this feeling most strongly. The rectory garden here is on a steep slope of the Mendips, looked after by the rector and his wife. The stone walls were being mended with his hands, the double-digging of an enormous vegetable plot was also his work. The delicious gooseberry fool was made from fruit from the garden.

It was essentially a family place, where three boys and two black Labradors could sport happily. It was also used for church affairs – a fête was imminent – and a lofty shed which once was used for drying teazles in the flourishing wool-trade days, stood ready for shelter should the heavens open on the great day.

Obviously, the rector and his wife were busy people, but everything was halted to welcome us, to discuss our problems, and to share their knowledge.

Looking down the valley to the church, with the

The garden at Brighstone Rectory on the Isle of Wight, whose famous incumbents include the seventeenth-century Thomas Kenn who, while pacing the Yew Walk, composed the hymns, 'Awake my soul and with the sun . . .' and 'Glory to thee, my God this night . . .' Two centuries later, Edward McAll was responsible for the building of the first lifeboat, and his curate, William Fox, became famous as an amateur palaeontologist, digging his fossils out of the nearby cliffs (including the Tyrannosaurus Rex now in the British Museum) and laying them out for assembly on the rectory lawn.

The rectory garden at Gawsworth in Cheshire, terraced and built with the house in 1707. Its terraces are stocked with roses, a rockery and a small annual bed, which lead steeply to a large lawned area planted to create a relaxed and visually 'soft' effect by its gardener, the Reverend Kenneth Povey.

flag of St. George flying against the hazy blue of Blagdon Lake, it was easy to understand the affection English people feel for their Church and those who serve it. The parish priest might have been there for many years, (thirty-six in the case of the rector of Yatton Keynell), or only one or two, but the tradition remains steadfast, despite the knowledge that he is only a temporary tenant of the house and garden.

The important part played by flowers in the life the church is reflected in this book, and it is evident that a great many have always been grown in the Vicarage gardens for the purpose of adorning the church, particularly at the times of the great church festivals.

In recent years, the popularity of flower festivals and garden open days has brought hundreds of people to visit churches and gardens, and has added much-needed support in the way of church funds.

But to the regular church-goer it is the familiar cycle of the church year which brings such satisfaction to the eye as he sits listening to the lessons, or the vicar's sermon, and notes the daffodils and lilies at Easter, the red and white flowers on the altar at Whitsun, and the holly, ivy and Christmas roses at the greatest of all the Church's festivals.

And what can be more satisfying than the bounty which surrounds him at Harvest Festival, when striped marrows jostle apples and tomatoes, the local baker's plaited loaves adorn the windowsills, and sheaves of corn stand triumphantly on the step up to the chancel. Here is God's blessing made manifest, the very Bread of Life, a glowing comfort to all men.

In contrast, during Holy Week, the bare altar, the stark lines of the pulpit, choir stalls and lectern, without leaf or flower to lift the spirits, brings to the worshipper the solemnity of that time of prayer.

The Reverend Francis Kilvert was particularly sensitive to flowers and their use in church ritual. In 1870, on Easter Eve, he describes minutely the church decorations in his Clyro church.

'Mrs. Morrell had been very busy all the morning preparing decorations for the Font, a round dish full of flowers in water, and just big enough to fit in the Font, and upon this large dish a pot filled and covered with flowers all wild, primroses, violets,

A plant paradise, the rectory garden at Diss in Norfolk.

wood anemones, wood sorrel, periwinkles, oxlips, and the first bluebells, rising in a gentle pyramid, ferns and larch sprays drooping over the brim . . .'

And later he describes a visit to the churchyard on the same day, when his parishioners came to deck the graves of their relatives.

'More and more people kept coming to the churchyard as they finished their day's work.

'At eight o' clock there was a gathering of the Choir in the Church. The moonlight came streaming in broadly through the chancel windows. As I walked down the Churchyard alone, the decked graves had a strange effect in the moonlight and looked as if the people had laid down to sleep for the night out of doors, ready dressed to rise early on Easter morning.'

This book has much to offer. It is a mine of botanical knowledge. It throws light on the complex and fascinating history of the Church and its surroundings. It touches on the debatable question of whether it is right to sell large old rectories and to replace them with small modern dwellings. Certainly, in this context, it is worth considering the loss of the heritage which these priceless old gardens can offer, something which can be lost for ever under the concrete and bricks of a new housing estate, for instance.

But perhaps the feeling we are left with, as we close the book, is the very Englishness of the whole project, and the affection which is felt by its many contributors for their own particular plot and for the joy they have in sharing it.

English vicarage gardens are indeed part of our way of life whether they are found in the countryside or among city wastes. We may never have visited one, but somehow we know exactly what a vicarage garden should be. This knowledge is a small piece of familiar awareness lodged at the back of our minds, and it sends a message of rightness, continuity and stability in a wavering world.

We respond instinctively to it, for it speaks to us of English history, endeavour and hope.

THE GARDEN AT
Lamorran

The Hon. Reverend John Townshend Boscawen

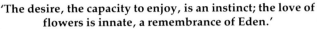

'The desire, the capacity to enjoy, is an instinct; the love of flowers is innate, a remembrance of Eden.'

Samuel Reynolds Hole

The Reverend Samuel Reynolds Hole, Rector of Caunton in Nottinghamshire between 1844 and 1887 and later Dean of Rochester, was the father of our *National Rose Society* and nursed a deep interest in England's most beautiful gardens, writing about many of them in numerous books and articles.

Of one garden in particular, the garden at Lamorran, a tiny village some 8 miles west of Truro in Cornwall, he reserved the highest praise. One spring day, having delivered a series of sermons and addresses as guest of the Cathedral in Truro, the Dean set off in the general direction of Lamorran without anything in his mind other than to enjoy a day off: 'Setting forth on a bright, sunny morning for a holiday, with the glad conviction that I had earned it, I had strolled for a couple of miles on the banks of the Fal – vessels from Norway unloading their great beams of timber on the right, and great bushes of golden furze and silver blackthorn showing on the left – when I saw on the opposite bank of the ferry at Malpas . . . a brother, whom I hardly knew beyond the repute which he has won in the floral world . . .'

The man he met was the Hon. Revd. John Townshend Boscawen, a member of the distinguished Cornish family that provides its Viscounts Falmouth. Together they walked towards Boscawen's home through the woods of Tregothnan, 'which must be charming indeed to sight and to scent when the honeysuckles, which climb to the very top of the trees are in flower and fragrance, and which were charming then in their early leafage, and with their primrose carpet below. And he showed me Tregothnan itself [the seat of Viscount Falmouth], the stately house and spacious gardens, with the camellias growing freely and flowering abundantly, as climbers on the walls and as shrubs in the open air, much as you see them in Southern France and Italy. Laurels also grown into great trees, and on either side of the broad drives and walks, with a wide margin of grass intervening, the rhododendrons! Then, for the first time, I saw these trees in their glory, beautiful pyramids, 15 to 20 feet in height, and covered from base to crown with great trusses of white and roseate, and crimson, and purple flowers. The taller trees of the shrubberies made an admirable background, and here and there the snowy blossoms of the cherry a most pleasing contrast. There is a grand old cork tree and many fine conifers, perhaps the best specimen of *Torreya myristica* in this country, and the most amiable *Amabilis* I ever saw . . . Then, as we walked from the park to the rectory my companion showed me, one mile to our right, the supposed site of the tomb of St. Geraint (Gerentius), and told him how, during the excavations of the antiquarian, they found withered bunches of flowers supposed to have been placed, as we place them now, in the grave, and how he collected the seed and sowed them in his garden, and these sleeping beauties woke up after a trance of thirteen centuries, to wit, since the days of King Arthur, and produced the same wild flowers, which ever since then, and I know not how long before, have sprung from Cornish soil.'

View of the creek from the bottom of the garden.

Wild honeysuckle climbs to the very top of the trees.

The site of the rectory at Lamorran is a hill facing south and south-west looking down on a sheet of water formed by the damming of a creek some hundred and fifty years ago. Since Boscawen's day the area of water, famed for its trout, has progressively decreased and where we look today upon mud withies and tree-grown swamp, would all have been open water then. On the hillside of this quiet, secluded valley, away from the beaten track of the busy world's highway, lay a storehouse of treasures. Boscawen's garden at Lamorran was 'Nature's Wild Garden' but every plant had a history and a pedigree, each chosen, and most planted, by Boscawen himself.

If indeed our love of flowers is 'a remembrance of Eden', our love of gardening an unconscious desire to re-create a vision of Paradise, then Boscawen's garden at Lamorran set a standard which, judged by this extract from Dean Hole's book (*A Book About the Garden*) and other contemporary reports, is unlikely to be surpassed.

'Believing in Eden as thoroughly as though I had seen it . . . believing that our love of horticulture and our happiness in a garden are reminiscences of our first glorious home, and longings to reproduce it . . . I shall never forget that "goodly place and goodly time" – the garden at Lamorran – and the joyous hours which passed so quickly there. It is indeed "a garden wild, but not without a plan", and that plan is to combine and blend Nature with art . . . so to diversify and surprise without incongruous or too sudden change, that the eye of the visitor should never weary, and that his steps, though upward, should never tire; but that increase of appetite should grow with that it fed on, and sigh, with the French lover, *trop n'est pas assez* . . . He has established, and long may he enjoy, the most perfect example of a wild garden, which, as I believe, is to be found in England.'

Gardening was in Boscawen's blood: in 1597 the Lord of Trewarthenick offered an ancestor of John Townshend Boscawen, one Nicholas Boscawen, the choice between money or some young apple trees growing in his nursery in exchange for certain rights Boscawen held over the Manor of Trewarthenick. Boscawen's ancestor chose the trees, professing himself 'an old foole that loved an apple', and set out at once with his servants and wain to fetch them. John would himself boast that he had been born a gardener and we know that his father (also a younger son of noble birth and thus also a clergyman) had given John, at an early age, a part of his garden at Wooton Rectory (near Dorking) to look after. In turn John instilled a love of beauty in his own son, Arthur, who was to become famous the world over for his rectory garden at Ludgvan in Cornwall. Though there was a time, it is said, when his father would let him do little more than rake the gravel paths at Lamorran.

Up until 1850 the garden at Lamorran was bare field. The first thing its creator did was to plant a belt of laurels so as to break the wind that rushed along the valley, over the water and up into the garden. A contemporary report in *The Gardener's Chronicle* describes how over the hillside Boscawen planted groups of *Pinus radiata* and *Thuja plicata* 'to make one hill look well from another'. As the contemporary woodcut shows, the Revd. Boscawen's idea was to integrate the garden with the surrounding countryside rather than plant an obviously cultivated plot in the midst of this stunning natural scenery. Besides the pines (magnificent examples by all accounts), there was a *Cupressus macrocarpa* 100 feet high. And the most notable among his palms was a *Chamaerops humilis*, planted by Boscawen in 1852. 'It has resisted many severe winters without protection, and now rears its head on high,' reports the *Chronicle*, 'unscathed by the fearful frosts of the last two winters. This is nearly, if not quite, the largest in England . . . Near it is a very fine specimen of *Sequoia sempervirens*, the red stringy bark of which is well shown.'

The trees, some of the largest species in the world, must have made an awesome sight. On the lowest part of the hill he planted hemlock spruces and a beautiful *Dacrydium franklinii*, the trees so happy that they appeared self-sown and thrived prosperously. These he 'interspersed with rhododendrons of every hue of the later hardier sorts.'

His Sikkim and rarer rhododendrons (including named hybrids raised by Boscawen: 'Lady of the Lake' and 'Rose of Falmorren') were planted higher up the hill in the shelter of two lines of conifers. In the same part Boscawen cut a horizontal shaft or

'*Our love of horticulture and our happiness in a garden are reminiscences of our first glorious home.*' Dean Hole
A woodcut of the garden made in 1881. Lamorran was a turning point in garden design. From 1849, long before William Robinson wrote his influential book, 'The Wild Garden', Boscawen set about creating what Dean Hole described as 'the most perfect example of a wild garden to be found in England.'

passage out of the hillside to grow alpines, and the resulting mound of earth (from which the woodcut view would have been obtained) was made a bed for a collection of rare crocuses.

Steps, made out of 'logs' of pine, lead the visitor up steep winding paths, 'past luxuriant plants of *Pieris formosa* with its lily-of-the-valley-like blossoms, and *Erica lusitanica*', to the 'Musa' garden. 'In this little amphitheatre are varieties of sedum, saxifrage, auricula, and many rock plants, including a variety of *Gentiana verna* with a white eye – a fine belt of rhododendrons surmounting them.'

The path out of the 'Musa' garden lead back down the hill, this time via its more western aspect and 'the lily walk' – 'fine specimens of that genus being

Boscawen's rhododendrons, now jungle plants 60 ft. or more in height.

planted at intervals with camellias.' *Cardiocrinum giganteum* (*syn. Lilium giganteum*) grew up to 12 feet high; Boscawen was one of the first to grow them *al fresco*.

Thence to a part of the garden which Boscawen called *Australis* because of the many eucalyptus, acacias and other plants from the Antipodes. Boscawen was one of the earliest English gardeners to benefit from the enormous influx of plants from foreign lands which occurred during the nineteenth century, and which were the materials with which the great tradition of the English Garden as we know it today grew and prospered. He owed his special connection with Australia and New Zealand to a marriage between one of his sisters and a member of the Dorrien Smith family in the Scilly Isles. In 1834, Augustus Smith arrived there from Hertfordshire,

where his reputation for being, in one of Boscawen's descendants' words, 'a somewhat bossy nobleman', had made him *persona non grata*. Once there, Smith set about creating the first compulsory system of education in Britain, and turned a smuggling fraternity into a community of pilots, who duly travelled the world, collecting seeds for what became the famous Abbey Gardens at Tresco. The mild climate of south-west England favours the growth of the many beautiful trees and flowering shrubs (hoherias, olearias, senecios and so on) that have found their way here from Australia and New Zealand, and both Boscawen and especially his son, Arthur (see *The Garden at Ludgvan*), were instrumental in their burgeoning popularity.

On the terrace below *Australis* stood twelve magnificent Irish Yews 'which were planted by Mr. Boscawen to disconnect the "wild garden" from the formal arrangement necessitated by the French bedding system, which for so many years was the rage, but which is now in a measure given up.'

Rather surprising this bedding feature in the midst of so natural a scene: apparently John's father was indirectly responsible for the incongruity. He had been the first to carry out the French system in England, though 'his son, as a boy, deeply regretted doing away with the old flowering shrubs at his home' to make way for it. Perhaps John had had a change of heart or perhaps it was some kind of memorial to his father. Whatever the case, it wasn't too long before – 'to the distress of the ladies' – all such instant colour disappeared from Lamorran.

John Townshend Boscawen was the first and last person to live in the rectory house, which was designed by an architect of Italian extraction, by the name of Vulliamy. Soon after his death, the house was taken down, stone by stone, and re-erected at Tresillian, the main church of the parish of Merther; and Merther and Lamorran were made one benefice (hardly surprising since in 1856 the Post Office Directory lists only eight households at Lamorran). Boscawen's garden was left to Nature, if ever it can truly be said to have been taken from Her.

Quoting from Thurston's famous book, *Cornish Parks and Gardens*, 'The grounds are now a wilderness. Some fine conifers, however, still survive.' The book is presently being up-dated by Dr. D. R. Hunt of Kew with help from Major E. W. M. Magor of St. Tudy in Cornwall, who reports that in 1985 they visited the site but, along with many others who have looked, 'had difficulty finding the place, and saw little sign of the conifers.' However, in the spring of 1987, guided by Nicholas Jeans of Lord

The house in which Boscawen lived at Lamorran.

Falmouth's Estate, and accompanied by the well-known Cornish horticulturist, the Reverend Ernest Saunders, we had more luck.

The road to Lamorran, down which Dean Hole and the Revd. Boscawen had walked one hundred years earlier, is still bound on either side by magnificent trees: specimens of oak, sycamore, beech, occasional plantings of fir, and beneath them, giant bushes of laurel and rhododendron, and ferns. Half a mile from the little church where Boscawen and his family are buried we could just make out his garden's outside wall and – thanks to our guide – Boscawen's old green garden gate, now almost swallowed up by rampant vegetation. The gate no longer opens but, climbing around it, we managed with great difficulty to force a path through dense trees and shrubs into what had been the outer limits of the rectory garden. Some few yards inside we emerged from undergrowth onto a path or driveway leading towards the little church, and clearly lined by the twelve ancient, and now gigantic, Irish yews which Boscawen had planted to separate his wild from formal gardens.

Looking up to the position from which the contemporary woodcut was made. Boscawen travelled a great deal, visiting his friends' gardens. On one occasion, when Boscawen was ill his doctor suggested he take a change of air. 'Where shall I go?' Boscawen asked. 'Stay at home,' the doctor replied.

The tiny Lamorran churchyard, where Boscawen lies buried.

Struggling on, we clung to giant roots as our guide led us up Boscawen's now treacherous, steep and winding paths, his pine-lined steps long gone. Hacking away at his rhododendrons and laurels that were now 'jungle' plants reaching 60 feet or more in height, we made out the original terraces which Boscawen had built to turn the hill into a garden. Stumbling on one of his flower-pots and picking up a fallen branch of his sequoia as souvenir, we paused for rest on the capping stones of a retaining wall.

Given the reports of the complete disappearance of the garden, it was a rare moment of discovery, perhaps of a sort which successful plant hunters feel in far-off lands. We had expected to find nothing, only wilderness, and we were all exhilarated. Here in the midst of tangled woodland, trees and shrubs towering 100 feet or more above us on the steep hillside, was clear evidence of the hand of Man. The thrill of discovery was inspired by a sense of contact with the past and what still remains of this almost legendary garden at Lamorran. But, more than this, there was a feeling that here had begun a great, characteristically English tradition of gardening, a tradition later to be described by William Robinson in his famous book *The Wild Garden*.

Eden – what might have been, had God drawn the best examples of His creation into a garden setting – had of course never existed. But Lamorran did, and came nearest to that idyll.

Beyond the site of the old house we came upon a vista majestically lined with conifers like giant trumpeters heralding the appearance of some great beauty. Was this the adit that Boscawen had carved for his alpine garden? Beyond it lay a mound terraced by a herringbone stone retaining wall. Was this where his rare collection of crocuses had grown? The enormous, nodding masts of fir seemed to us to murmur assent; or was it merely discontent at our clumsy disturbance of their long, peaceful sleep.

Bitton

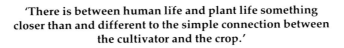

The Reverend Canon Henry Nicholson Ellacombe

'There is between human life and plant life something closer than and different to the simple connection between the cultivator and the crop.'

Many clergyman used their gardens in their pastoral work not just as convenient places to hold parish functions but as examples of God's handiwork, and the finest nineteenth-century record of this is contained in Canon Ellacombe's writings about his vicarage garden at Bitton in Gloucestershire (now Avon), where he was vicar from 1850.

In fact, Henry Nicholson Ellacombe with his father before him accounted for nearly a century of stewardship of Bitton, and in 1916, *Country Life* described father and son as 'two of the great master gardeners of the world.' Among his friends, Canon Ellacombe numbered many of the greatest horticulturalists of the day, and William Robinson described Bitton as the ideal example 'of a quiet, peaceful garden of grass and trees and simple borders . . . every nook and corner has its appropriate flower, in a word, it is just such a garden as one would expect a scholar to possess who has sympathy for all that lives and breathes . . .'

'The Canon was a great gardener,' wrote his biographer A. W. Hill. 'But we must interpret that word as implying something more than the faculty of getting plants to grow. He was pre-eminent in that, but what struck me more was his love for them, his intimacy with them and their peculiarities.'

This 'intimacy' was nowhere better expressed than in the introduction he wrote for *Flowers and Gardens*, a book written by Forbes Watson and published posthumously. Forbes Watson was a surgeon, artist and naturalist, a man noted by Ellacombe for his faculty of close observation and patience in research. As a student of botany he had become very interested in the scientific structure of plants and how they functioned, but later became dissatisfied with a perspective which failed to explain their beauty. Canon Ellacombe wrote: 'He could not stop there, he was a deeply religious man, and he felt that nothing was made in vain, and that the beauty of leaf and flower had *its* functions, and was as necessary to the life of the plant as any other part of it.'

Forbes Watson made a distinction between what he called the sensuous and non-sensuous pleasure that we receive from flowers. By 'sensuous' he meant a flower's colour, shape, smell, juiciness, wiriness, softness, hardness, sharpness. The Canon explains: 'The scent of the rose is delicious, even on a handkerchief, and altogether independently of its connection with the flower; and the blue of the larkspur would charm us on the painter's palette. But so far we please nothing but sense, we stop at the outside; the plant is no more than a bundle of qualities. For true appreciation we must advance beyond this, and think of the plant as a living being – a friend whom we may love, and whose character must be intimately known. We shall wish to learn all we can of it, the time of its appearance and flowering, what it does with itself in the winter, whether dropping its leaves and standing bare-branched like a tree or shrub, or disappearing beneath the ground like a snowdrop or hyacinth, or facing the cold with a tuft of leaves lying close upon the earth like a foxglove. What sort of locality does it love – field, rock or marsh? How does it treat other plants when it encounters them? Does it twine round them like a convolvulus, creep over them like many trailing plants, or bear itself erect like a buttercup? How does it wither? shabbily and untidily like the pansy, or in the neat decorous mode of the gentianella? These and all other facts which we can learn about a plant have a value in an imaginative point of view; they tell us something about it, and so enable us to understand it, to read its true meaning and character. And we find that the sensuous qualities have more than a sensuous value, for the imagination discovers that they are but a symbolic language, which we must receive as exponent of the hidden nature of a flower, just as the features of the human countenance are interpreters of the mind within.'

How the clergyman can make use of his garden in his main work, Ellacombe does not dictate. In his book, *In A Gloucestershire Garden* he wrote, 'the method that would be very useful in the hands of one would be perfectly useless in the hands of another. I would only say generally, that the love of flowers and gardening is so universal amongst the English peasantry that a country parson will often find a better introduction to a cottager through his garden than by any other means.' It was once said of Ellacombe that his 'favourite doctrine was that a true gardener is known by the pleasure he takes in giving plants to his friends and judged by that standard he was a prince among gardeners.' On the one hand Ellacombe recognised that 'it is impossible to get or keep a large collection [of plants] except by constant liberality in giving – "There is that scattereth, and yet increaseth," was Solomon's experience,' – but he also realised that 'the parson who is liberal with his plants will find the increase not only in the pleasant intercourse with his neighbours, but also in the enlargement of his own garden, which thus spreads beyond his own fences into the gardens of the cottages.'

In the same book, Ellacombe tells us of 'the great lesson that our gardens teach us . . . that everything in nature is subject to the strictest law, for this is taught by plants almost more surely than by anything else . . . the plant-world is governed by strict, unchanging, and, we must say, eternal laws. What I mean is this: If I take two sets of small seeds in my hands, they may at first sight seem absolutely the same, yet one may be the seed of a small annual, the other the seed of a large tree; and if I know the history of the plants that produced the seeds, I can foretell with certainty the whole future life of the seeds, the shape and nature of the leaves, the size of the plants, the colours of the flowers, the shapes and uses of the fruit, and the length of life which will be allotted to each. Every plant that grows is produced and lives by the strictest law; like has produced like from the beginning, and will do so to the end.' Man's varieties are strictly defined, even 'the wild pelargonium, from which our numberless varieties have sprung, may still be found at the Cape . . . and though the gardeners have so much altered [it] that it is now a flower with five almost equal petals, yet the original irregular form cannot be entirely obliterated, and the one larger petal of the typical plant is always shown by the curious hole at the base, which no hybridising has completely destroyed, but the use of which has never been satisfactorily accounted for.'

What then of the garden itself? 'It is not a large garden – the whole extent, including a good proportion of lawn, being about an acre and a half, and in shape a parallelogram, or double square. It lies on the west side of the Cotswolds, which rise about half a mile away to the the height of 750 feet; and about 15 miles to the south are the Mendips. These two ranges of hills do much to shelter us from the winds, both from the cold north and easterly winds and from the south-west winds, which in this part of England are sometimes very violent. I attach great importance to this kindly shelter from the great strength of the winds, for plants are like ourselves in many respects, and certainly in this, that they can bear a very great amount of frost if only the air is still, far better than they can bear less cold if accompanied with a high wind. The garden then has this advantage of shelter; it has also the advantage of a good aspect, for though the undulations are very slight, the general slope faces the south; and it has the further advantage of a rich and deep alluvial soil, which, however, is so impregnated with lime and magnesia, that it is hopeless to attempt rhododendrons, azaleas, kalmias, and a host of other things; and it has the further disadvantage of being only about 70 feet above the sea-level, which makes an insuperable difficulty in the growth of the higher Alpines. On the whole, the garden is favourable for the cultivation of flowers, and especially for the cultivation of shrubs, except those which dislike the lime.'

Much to William Robinson's taste, there was nothing formal about the Canon's plantings – no overall plan, no design. He put a plant in the place in which it would live most happily, and changed his composition of plants constantly. His garden, he explained, 'has grown into its present shape and plan, and has almost formed itself; and I may say with certainty that though I have many trees, shrubs, and other plants which have been in their present places for many years – many over seventy years – yet there is not a single path or flower-bed that is the same now as it was thirty or even twenty years ago. And this adds much to the pleasure of a garden; this power of altering to suit the wants of growing trees and

The Canon and Ferula glauca.

shrubs . . . or to suit one's own peculiar taste or fancy.'

It was his habit to show his visitors the same way around the garden, beginning at the porch on the south side of the house, and enchanting them with stories about his plants: 'There are trees on my lawn which were planted when children were born; there are hundreds of plants which tell me of the liberal

View of the church that Ellacombe would have had from his garden seat beneath the ancient yews. Below, the fern-leaved beech.

help given by such gardens as Kew, Edinburgh, Dublin, and many other public gardens, both British and foreign; there are hundreds of others which speak to me of delightful private gardens, and of the pleasant freemasonry that exists among true gardeners; there are flowers which tell of pleasant travels, and long walks, and beautiful spots which I shall probably never see again; there are others which bring to memory voices which I shall never hear, and faces which I shall never see again in this world; and hundreds more which in their several ways have their own memories, and their own associations, which make each and all forget-me-nots of the highest value and beauty.'

A. W. Hill recalls that one of Ellacombe's favourite diversions for first-time visitors was a great oak which still stands at the south east corner of the vicarage garden: he would 'ask an opinion of its age. With some knowledge of the soil and rates of growth at Bitton I guessed it at 150 years. Some would guess it at 200 years, some at 300. He would then tell you he planted it himself. He would also tell you how anxious a local timber merchant was to buy it, the same man who, as an inducement to the Canon to part with it, offered to put by enough boards cut out

of it to make his coffin!' The garden's owner today, Mr. Michael Ashbee, pointed out other trees that have survived, among them a huge fern-leaved beech part-way down the garden on the south side, 'which,' the Canon held, 'makes a beautiful lawn tree, and has lovely tints both in spring and autumn'. Today the

beech helps to obscure two ancient yews growing near together, some yards closer to the boundary wall. Here, at their feet, the Canon would sit on his favourite wooden bench (the remains of which still survive beneath an almost impenetrable canopy of leaves), and from which he would then have had a clear view of the church beyond the garden's boundary wall.

One hundred years ago, he wrote that 'far beyond the memory of the oldest inhabitant [the yews] have carried a swing, and it is pleasant to think to how many generations of the children of the village these yew trees with their swing have been a never-failing delight. They are represented in an old painting quite 200 years old.' There remains evidence – large boulder stones – of a rock walk beneath these three trees, and a ginkgo, the only survivor of a number that had, in Ellacombe's time, seeded themselves in the garden.

Still standing too is his magnificent tulip tree, set on the lawn not far away from two magnolias to which it is botanically allied. Its large, quaintly shaped leaves, which in autumn turn to a rich yellow and brown, and its handsome, sweet-scented flowers, make it very attractive . . .' Alas, the *Catalpa bignonioides*, illustrated here, that stood on the lawn nearer the house, is no more. Ellacombe loved its

'trusses of beautiful white and purple flowers, which are unlike any other', but admitted that being so short in leaf (July until the first frosts) it has its drawback as a lawn tree, and it seems subsequent owners agreed with him.

Behind the tulip tree and shrub border on the north side he grew apples, plums, cherries and pears,

The yews, over 300 years old.

The catalpa bearing fruit, and Chusan palm by the vicarage. See how it has grown (our picture, page 25) since Ellacombe planted it over 100 years ago.

A waxy, sweet-scented flower of Ellacombe's tulip tree.

and holly trees, and on the west boundary by the schoolhouse, can still be seen one of his palms.

For the plantsman the first part of his book, *In My Vicarage Garden and Elsewhere*, provides a fascinating record of the garden in the year 1900, and it is clear that from the beginning of the flowering year there was always something of great beauty and interest: 'Spring is the time at which flowers wake out of their sleep,' the Canon wrote, 'and the awakening takes place, not according to months, or even to weather, but according to the needs and nature of each different plant.' Among the first that year were the early crocuses, *C. imperati* and *C. stellaris*, and his favourite snowdrops, which still, today, cover the ground as assuredly each January as they did then – 'when one begins to speak of the crocus and snowdrop, it is hard to know when to stop.' Also in January the Christmas roses and winter aconites, and the ground coverers, *Cyclamen coum* and *Asarum europeum*, maintain the link with winter, the latter covering 'the ground closely especially in dense shade ... and it will even produce its curious, though inconspicuous, flowers in the depth of winter.'

Among his first flowering shrubs came *Clematis cirrhosa*, *Garrya elliptica*, *Chimonanthus praecox* and *Lonicera fragrantissima*. On swept spring with his favourite rich deep blue-flowering, broad-petalled *Iris unguicularis*, narcissi, tulips and, among his flowering shrubs, 'sheets of white' laurustinuses, *Chaenomeles japonica*, *Photinia serrulata*, 'a special beauty of its own in its young shoots, which at a very short distance look like fine flowers,' and, growing against the house, *Forsythia suspensa*, 'like a golden curtain at least 15ft high'.

Crocus imperati.

Asarum europeum.

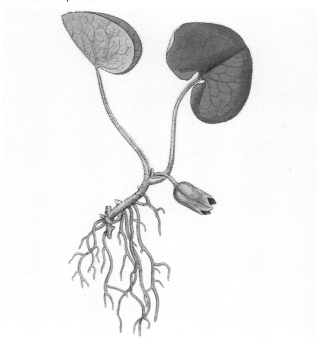

Clematis cirrhosa.

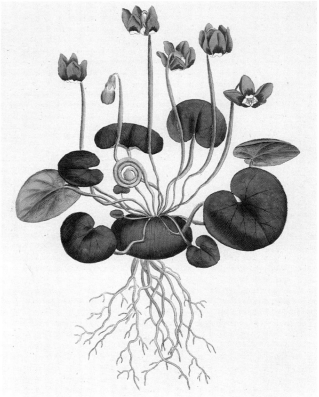

Cyclamen coum.

Then came the magnolias 'loaded with flowers . . . I think the spring of 1900 will be memorable in many ways in the garden. I cannot remember a season in which flowers were so abundant on almost every flower-bearing plant.'

Chimonanthus praecox.

Among his roses, in summer, he makes special mention of *R. hemisphaerica*: 'on one of my bushes grown against a wall, I must have had nearly 200 blooms, more or less open at the same time; really a grand sight.' Of the herbaceous plants, the larkspurs were very grand, 'and even such moisture-loving plants were quite happy in spite of the drought'. Of his flowering shrubs, the wistarias, 'both white and blue, almost recalled the pictures that we have seen of them as grown in the gardens of Japan, where they are special favourites,' the Christ's thorn (*Paliurus spp.*) 'was a sheet of pale gold and was, I think, more beautiful in my own garden than where I saw it in its wild habitats in North Italy.' (The Canon would take his holidays in Europe each year, collecting plants in a handkerchief tied to an alpenstock, taking with him such holiday reading as the works of Horace and *Tourist's Flora*.)

'But if I were to pick out the shrub that has more especially distinguished itself this summer, I should pick out the *Rhus cotinus* (syn. *Cotinus coggygria*, the Venetian Sumach or Smoke Tree) . . . The great beauty of the tree is in its flowering . . . the

Photinia serrulata.

Iris unguicularis.

whole shrub is covered with panicles of abortive flowering stems, in which the true flowers are entirely absent, and nothing remains but the stems. Yet those bundles of flower stems form the most beautiful vegetable feathers, resembling marabout feathers.'

Aster amellus was, in 1900, the earliest autumn plant to flower – 'this year it was crowded with Red Admirals and occasional Humming Bird moths,' and among his crocuses – 'the one that has made itself most at home is *C. pulchellus*, a lovely pale blue with white anthers.' His autumn flowering shrubs included *Abelia chinensis*, with its reddish-brown stems and abundance of small white flowers, and the half-shrubby *Phygelius capensis*, with its pretty scarlet blooms. He finds nothing depressing in twilight months of the flowering year, autumn is 'the great point at which all plants gradually arrive, and which is really the true object of their existence . . . To me it seems that the autumn colours of tree foliage are absolutely a fixed mark of the tree as the colour of the flowers and to some extent even more so.'

Special mention is made of the brilliant orange-red scarlet colouring of his *Parrotia persica*, and the ginkgo for its 'rich colour which begins at the lowest branch of the tree and works upwards (with most other trees the course is different)', and the brilliantly coloured foliage of *Rhus cotinoides* (*syn. Cotinus americanus*), which 'was by far the most beautiful of all autumnal shrubs.'

November, the month which he advises is the easiest for moving plants around, sees Canon Ellacombe plotting and re-plotting. The Canon was averse to fixed plans, rigidly adhered to, however good and beautiful. 'Every garden is subject to many changes . . . I have always noticed that the more a man loves his garden, the more he delights in constantly changing the arrangements, which were, perhaps, good for a time.'

THE GARDEN AT
Topcliffe

Canon and Mrs. W. C. Slade

'What do I find amongst all this? What I personally find in gardening is an atmosphere for prayer. I find it a marvellous situation for intercession.'

The house at Topcliffe, near Thirsk in North Yorkshire, an inauspicious bungalow with all the characterlessness of 1960s' English architecture, was built in the orchard of the old vicarage. Centuries of fallen apples might at least have provided fruitful soil, but it had to contend with mounds of builders' rubbish and is, at best, 'very average'. Of the many great trees as well as fruit trees that were rooted out to build the vicarage, only one lime and a beech remain. Nevertheless, with the inspired confidence that you might expect from the spiritual advisor to the district, Canon Slade, and his wife Elizabeth, a professional horticulturalist who trained at *The Royal Horticultural Society* garden at Wisley, have together made a virtue out of their situation by perfectly blending new and old (they share the ancient garden wall with the old vicarage) and by creating a site of real meditative tranquillity for their many appreciative visitors. Canon Slade explains:

'When we came I was very conscious of the difference between the old vicarage and this one. I knew I had to do something with the outhouses; they are the link.'

'The main idea, the main plan, emerged from my work as spiritual adviser to the area. I use this room for interviews, to talk to people and counsel them. To look out of its big picture window at the garden relaxes me, and sitting here and looking out across the front garden to the Pennines, way in the distance, helps those who come out from the towns and cities to talk. In her choice of plants and in her planning, Elizabeth has consciously tried to create something that people can relax with; she feels this is part of her ministry. The people who come to talk to me also get fed of course, get cups of tea, and Elizabeth is responsible for that too – but she has always tried to create an atmosphere in the garden that is very much a part of the whole job. This view is the first thing people see when they drive up here and stop – and a lot of them do just stop and look. And wonder. And it has an effect on their attitude when they come into the house.

'When we came I was very conscious of the difference between the old vicarage and this one, recalls Mrs. Slade. I knew that I had to do something with the outhouses. They are the link; they are a focal

The herbaceous border.

point not to be covered up. Similarly the wall – the colours of the brick in that wall, especially at night as the sun is setting, are simply magnificent. Cover them with plants, yes, but don't hide them. Wherever you go – that way onto the Pennines or the other way onto the moors, there are grey stone walls and villages. This is quite different, a sort of oasis of brick in the Vale of York.

'At the start we had a retired army man called Howard to do the actual digging; he was very enthusiastic about digging things out and clearing the ground, which is just what I wanted . . . until to my horror he dug up the weigela which I only just

managed to rescue from the bonfire. We arrived in August 1982 and he came in twice a week until November when the clearing was finished.

'One feature of the garden climate which has influenced us is a howling westerly wind coming straight from the Pennines. We are the first thing it hits. We keep a close eye on the direction of both wind and sun when planting, but we haven't actually built anything to screen the wind because we do not want to lose the view. With the combination of wind and extremely low temperatures in the winter of '85 I lost more than ever before. Most winters are not as costly.

'The only other principle of planning has been to plant for the least amount of work, so that whoever takes this garden on when we leave is not going to be landed with intensive cultivations.

'Once we had cut the lawns, front and back, they more or less presented the shape of the garden as it is today, except that we dug out the shape of the herbaceous border and the heather garden in the front. Howard, dear gentleman, cut it out as a rectangle. And when I gave him some stones to edge it and protect the heathers from my son's car as it backed out of the garage, he put them in vertically so when we looked out of the window the plot looked like a dog's graveyard!

'After working at Wisley and *The Royal Horticultural Society* offices in London in my teens, and taking the RHS exam, I did a thesis on rock gardening. To this day my husband says I have stone disease because I cannot go past an interesting piece without wanting to pick it up. Indeed, our rock garden progressed from what stone we had already gathered, as well as what we could plant – we don't get a great deal of sun on the north side of the old vicarage wall so there is nothing particularly delicate.

'The rock garden includes: 3 conifers – *Picea abies* "Pumila", *Thuja* "Rheingold", *Juniperus communis* "Compressa"; aubrieta, *Alyssum saxatile*, *Primula denticulata*; many bulbs: crocus, aconites, dwarf tulips and miniature daffs, *Anemone blanda*, *Iris reticulata* (the dark purple, very pale blue and yellow ones); various alpine pansies and sweet violets, cowslips and three varieties of campanula; a dwarf veronica shrub; pale pink and dark rose coloured thrift; miniature roses; dwarf dianthus and various sedums and sempervivums; *Potentilla nitida* "Rubra"; *Phlox subulata* (pink and blue varieties), wild primroses, various saxifragas, sun roses (*Helianthemum spp.*), thyme (bush cushion and encrusted varieties), pink and white rock roses (*Cistus spp.*) and white double arabis.

'Progressing west along the north side of the garden there are some redcurrant bushes which I have made into bays with grass on three sides so that you can sit up against the wall. Then comes the buddleia and a cut-out bed for shrubs where you'll find potentilla, escallonia, spiraea, together with pansies (which do tremendously well in this garden) and polyanthus. Our deutzia was beautiful this year, a very pale pink literally fountaining down in front of my precious weigela, its own darker pink complementing the green and the colours of the old brick wall. We also have a philadelphus and nearby a lonicera spills over from the old vicarage.

'Then we come to the beech tree, survivor of the original garden, which has bulbs beneath it: crocus, daffodils, and a bulb which has obviously been there for a tremendous length of time but which I simply cannot identify. It comes after the daffodils, a very pale greeny cream with the growth of a bluebell on a long stem, but upright with no hanging head.

'And then along the west boundary are Scotch pine, rugosa roses (a lovely selection of dark red,

Above, the rock garden; below, the cut-out bed for shrubs.

pink and white), holly, flowering cherry, forsythia and a blue cedar. Up the south side, the most productive section of the garden, are the raspberry canes and a strawberry bed with a rowan tree, and lavender bushes. I have two sweet pea columns and some runner bean columns, and nearer the house planted a fir to break the expanse of empty, empty grass.

'Then we come to the herb garden and the rhubarb, and we're back in the front garden.

'What do I find amongst all this? What I personally find in gardening is an atmosphere for prayer – I find it a marvellous situation for intercession. You are on your knees most of the time, weeding; you haven't really got to use your brain too much, it being a fairly repetitive job sometimes, and I do find it a tremendous time for intercession. And the other point is that as a woman I spend a great deal of my time cleaning the house and keeping it tidy, only to see someone immediately come in and kick it all about; there's nothing really creative about house-work. Whereas in the garden, although a certain amount is bothering about weeds and so forth, it is also a creative activity. You are creating something that is going to last. If you put in a shrub it is going to be there for years.'

As if to emphasise the connection between their faith and the garden, Canon Slade points to a garden hut at the south end of the vicarage. 'That's a chapel. Normally at this time of year (July) Elizabeth has it all planted up with petunias but she's saving the pennies this year. All around it in the spring are daffodils, snowdrops, polyanthus and pansies. We had to have a place because there was nowhere in the

house for me to hear confessions and so on. So when I left my last parish I ordered it without asking the price. I knew I really had to have it. Then, when I left

The sin bin: 'A chapel where I hear confessions, surrounded in the spring by daffodils, snowdrops, polyanthus and pansies.'

the parish, I was presented with a cheque for £335, and someone who comes to me said, "I hear you want a hut, so here's a cheque for £100." When I got the bill it was for exactly £435. So you see, it was meant to happen!'

THE GARDEN AT
Barton-le-Clay

The Reverend Ian Graham-Orlebar

'Vicarage gardens are places of renewal, of refreshment. This is what the Church is best at, indeed what people look to the Church for. Yet sadly, it is precisely what the Church these days forgets.'

Just off the M1 on the way to Luton, and thence along the busy A6, lies the village of Barton-le-Clay. It is so anonymous in appearance that you can easily travel past without granting it a second look. In fact the part of the village which straddles the road is Barton's relatively modern extension. Not immediately obvious to today's traveller are the older cottages, church and rectory, tucked out of sight – the original village which, despite the encroachment of the twentieth century, has managed to retain its timeless, English country atmosphere. Ian Graham-Orlebar and his mother, Mrs. Graham, take us on a tour of the rectory garden, just as they do when they open it to the public on selected days under the National Gardens Scheme.

'I have been here for sixteen years, and my mother joined me three years after I arrived. The garden is about 2 acres of land with a spring-fed moat, though as we shall see it is now boosted artificially by a pump. Rainwater passes easily through the Chiltern chalk but when it hits the Bedfordshire clay the water stops abruptly and gushes out into my garden. Had I known at the start what I do now, I would have dredged the moat. In hot summers it's a real problem – too shallow; and in the summer of '76 it dried up altogether.

'Basically the garden is flat, with the rectory along most of its northern boundary, its southern boundary running parallel to a public footpath. I always say that anyone is welcome to come and look around, but don't peer in or push through or walk out with flowers – it does sometimes happen.

'My predecessor wasn't a gardener and the place hadn't really been kept up since the war when two gardeners attended it. So, when I arrived, it was a wilderness. There was a fallen tree across the lawn and weeds everywhere, bindweed like spaghetti in the flower beds.

'The first job was to cut down fifty dead elms to give us a clear view of the Chiltern hills, southwards across the garden; we had contractors in to do that. Interestingly, the first hill, unnaturally steep, attracts a number of geologists who come and dig about. In 1906 during the well-known *Daily Mail* air race, London to Birmingham, an aeroplane staggered over the hill and crashed here. The pilot got out, uninjured, and the rector invited the man to join him for breakfast. He stayed for a week while the village

The view south across the moat towards the Chiltern hills.

Looking North towards rectory and church, from the moat walk.

carpenter tried to repair the plane. In the end it took off but crashed again, this time in the next field, and had to be dismantled.

'The next thing was to clear the flower beds of the most dreadful ground elder. 'Never let it see a Sunday' is my motto. The cure for bindweed and ground elder is to snap it off; even if you can't pull it up, snap it off, repeatedly, and then it will die.

'Then came the flame-thrower. For clearing up dead weeds there's nothing to beat one, or so I thought. There was the most terrible growth of dead ivy up the walls, and the flame-thrower seemed the natural answer. But up it went – whoosh – all at once! It was very frightening and almost set the rectory on fire.

'Next we started the compost; we're great composters, and we have a horse – that helps! I have four heaps altogether, all dated: this year, last year etc.; dated and regularly turned. Each heap, each year, must represent about a ton of compost. I'll say to a choirboy (a largish choirboy) "£5 if you turn this heap onto that empty one." And he generally starts off with great enthusiasm . . . But it's all or nothing on a job like that: "£5 for the whole job but nothing if you partly do it."

'We put the compost onto the garden first thing in the spring, all around everything, never digging it in, just leaving it on top. Within a month or two you wouldn't know that it had been laid down; it just disappears. The soil – all chalky clay – is so hungry that it consumes everything.

'There's a good bit of technicalia here: everybody always says never put your weed-killed grass mowings onto the compost heap. But actually it doesn't matter a bit if they are allowed to rot for about six months. Whether one or two things that died might not have done, I'm not sure, but there is definitely a principle in there somewhere – "Try things out and see how they work, whatever the books say."

Tobacco plants (nicotiana), backed by asters and irises, all doing well despite being in the shade of a copper beech.

The West bed, 'Paxton's territory – the nearest we get to a traditional herbaceous border.'

The Methodist bridge leading from the grotto to the moat walk.

'If I have an obsession, it must be the grass on the main lawn. We scarify it in the spring; they say that if you do it in the autumn the plants tiller better – divide and spread better – so perhaps it is best to do it both in spring and autumn. We've got one of those marvellous Black and Decker, very fast scarifiers, and then we puncture it with a revolving machine attached to a ride-on mower. Finally we use a Walkover (a sort of spray machine) for putting on fertiliser, having learnt that it is much cheaper to use liquid fertiliser. It used to cost £100 to do the lawns with the granular type, but now we use liquid phostrogen and seaweed every three weeks. You see, if you want to kill moss you must feed the grass. Other than that, the lawn is given its freedom – enough for it to dip into hollows as much as it likes,

The formal patch to the east of the rectory.

just so long as it isn't scalped by the mowing machine.

'Having decided to open up the garden, to change the focus by removing the trees, we had created a design which takes the eye out of the garden. Another design principle concerned my ausblicks: as you walk round the garden you'll suddenly see little 'windows' onto other views. Finally, there is the whole question of the relationship of the house to the garden, which we have tried to solve in our plant planning. Have you noticed that at Hidcote there's no relationship between the two? You cannot see the house from the garden or the garden from the house; it's most extraordinary.

'I am the designer and my mother is the "plantsman". If she says we must have a *Euphorbia myrsinites*, she'll have one but she won't really mind where it fits into the overall scheme. She'll know what conditions it likes, but has no idea of the overall view. You see, I'm Capability Brown to her Paxton.'

The Lower Lawn
With her thorough knowledge of plants Mrs. Graham is not perturbed by the challenge of a chalk-laden soil. 'I was lucky, I had an old aunt who had all the Gertrude Jekyll books and I wish to goodness I could have got them from her, but I did study them very

closely. Of course Jekyll's was so much the herbaceous style of gardening and sadly we can do little of that here. The nearest to a traditional herbaceous border is, I suppose, the west bed, though it's really at its best in the autumn: dahlias, chrysanthemums and so on.

'Here for the summer are the phlox and the lilies that make such a good view as you walk into the garden. We have already had a lot of lilies; now in August here is a second batch which I'm rather pleased about. I went out of my way to have two types of lily, an early and a late one. Also because I had to choose only lime-tolerant ones, and I like low ones in the front, it takes a lot of working out. At that stage I am 100% plantsman. The colourful green and cream-leaved plant is a variegated brunnera, and what makes it such a good plant to have here is that it keeps the lily bulbs cool. The rose at the back is "Nevada".'

The Formal Garden
To the east of the rectory (still on the north border of the garden) lies the only formal patch – beds of roses laid in formal patterns overlooked by an eighty-year-old "Cupid" rose on the house wall, at whose feet grow an unusual combination of irises (*Iris sibirica*) striking foils for ground cover lamiums (*Lamium maculatum*).

Three R. 'Ballerina' tumble over an old tree stump; in the foreground Ligularia 'The Rocket' and a red astilbe defy the steep bank by being firmly bedded in the rector's shelf beds. 'To make a shelf bed you simply bang in posts and fill up the gap between them and the bank,' he says.

'We're both interested in silver plants and you'll see some here,' the rector continues. 'Every year we go to the Royal Show and re-stock from Ramparts Nurseries.

'And that's pineapple broom in the corner (*Cytisus battandieri*) – it smells and looks like a pineapple and is covered in June. And the rose? Well, someone said if you've only got room for one climber rose, choose "Compassion", and I would agree – lovely rose.'

The Upper Garden
'Near the shade of the copper beech lies a bed of asters, tobacco plants and irises where once there were roses. The irises come through all right because they're well out before any shade appears from the copper beech in June. Then there is the bed of hellebores and Solomon's Seal. They flower in the spring before there are any leaves on the beech, and anyway they like shade and are altogether as happy as can be.

'In springtime, beneath the beech and spreading

yew, we have daffodils and bluebells, and we've got some rather nice white bluebells which show up very well. The two trees mark the dividing line between flower garden and what was once a kitchen garden. We planted many of the trees here on the top lawn – silver birches, hornbeam – and the two flower beds are 'colour to be seen at a distance': tobacco plants and annual mallows in the first. One doesn't often walk over here, but it's a rather important focal point looking from the house, so we have tried for something that can be seen from a long way off. The other bed is packed with delphiniums, as my mother is a member of *The Delphinium Society*. This year, for the first time, we have staked them with wire hoops. Last year we had eighty canes in here, and we said never again. Less unsightly and only twenty hoops are required to do the same job.

The Moat Walk
'Now we come to the south boundary of the top lawn. There's wild old philadelphus, and the hedge maples that we planted – perhaps unwisely – some fifteen years ago. They've come up to form a marvellous grotto. Come in!

'Do you see what I mean? We've got a completely different atmosphere in here. Can you hear the

spring? Years ago we got the choirboys to dig for a week and work a sludge pump to pull up the mud and the water. And they dug and they pumped and they loved it. Even the television people came in to watch them. The spring now fills the enormous hole which they dug, and an artificial pump takes the water out and feeds it over a waterfall into the moat.

'It's almost pitch dark here yet there are things that will grow: hostas, ferns, Solomon's Seal, and lily of the valley. I love this spot. The bridge was built in the year of the Jubilee; a chap in the village, called Dennis Hibberd, had the archways built from windows of a Methodist church in Hitchin that had been pulled down to make way for Sainsbury's. A Tarzan's rope used to hang down from a tree to the moat, but once I caught the choirboys swinging on it during a half-hour break between two weddings . . .'

Both obviously derive an enormous personal satisfaction from the garden they have created together, but as Ian is keen to stress, 'Our main thing is making the garden a useful place. More often than not it is swarming with people. In a minute someone

'The parsonage gate should always be open, and every parishioner welcomed; there need be no fear of any undue advantage being taken of the free permission to enter – the one difficulty will be to induce them to come in.' Canon Ellacombe, 1895.

will come from the churchyard to walk around here and sit in a chair. I say to all the old people, do pop in and use it – come! I'm sure that that must have been the intention of the original vicarage gardens.

'We always plan the church fête to open in the middle of July because that's when the roses will be out. And today we're planning for the arrival on Sunday of a group of disabled children who are coming for a riding holiday; hence the marquee and the Portaloo. The boys sleep in the hall, and then there are tents for the rangers.

'Of course another feature of this being a rectory garden is that we will not always be able to live here, but I do not let that affect my gardening. And my mother would never not plant something for fear of not seeing it flower; if she likes it she will have it. But I will be furious with my successor if he doesn't keep it up – he will be chosen purely with that in mind.'

THE GARDEN AT
Childswickham

The Reverend and Mrs. Anthony Lee

**'It's important that one isn't solely concerned with ideas,
even though they may be important ideas concerned with
the spiritual life of people in the parish . . . I find it a very
sobering act to work this plot of land.'**

'When a house is described as "like an ordinary English parsonage", we know at once what it
means. We picture to ourselves a building of moderate size – not pretentious – neither a mansion
nor a suburban villa . . . and of an old foundation; yet with many additions and accretions of
different dates, each bearing some impress of the successive owners; and the garden is of the same
character, often standing (and always in the ideal parsonage garden) near the church and
churchyard, so that the church forms the feature in the garden. The parsonage garden is not large,
seldom exceeding two acres, and more often not exceeding one, with little glass, and no pretention
to a high-class garden, but with a good spread of old lawn and many old trees and flowering
shrubs, all suggestive of repose and quiet, pleasant shade, and freedom from the bustle of the
outside world.'

It might seem unlikely that Canon Ellacombe's abstraction of the characteristics of 'the English
vicarage' should be expressed precisely in a particular example, but, in this respect at least, the
vicarage at Childswickham, near Broadway in the Cotswolds, happily defies all expectations of
probability.

Childswickham vicarage is a composite house, a rambling, higglety-pigglety mixture whose well-documented record over 600 years speaks volumes of village history. In 1303, in a document sanctioning the transference of tithes from the then rector to Bordesley Abbey, the Bishop made it a condition that the Abbey should provide for a vicar of the parish and that a vicarage be built, the present-day site of which is then described: 'There is a garden on church soil on the west enclosed with hedges and ditches lying between the house on one side and a mill pond on the other.' The original house would have been timbered and thatched. Whether it survived as originally built until the sixteenth century is not clear, but in 1569 the vicar was defendant in a case in the Consistory Court for allowing it to become ruinous, and in Elizabethan times it was replaced by the central wattle and daub section of what is now the vicarage. Early in the nineteenth century two vicars pleaded to be allowed to dwell elsewhere, one on account of the 'vicarage being a mere cottage and unfit for our residence', and it fell to two later incumbents, John Hartley from 1861 and Robert Hilaro Barlow during his incumbency from 1875 to make the improvements, alterations, and additions which form the property of today.

The vicarage garden, near church and churchyard (the solid tower and graceful spire as Ellacombe decreed, forming the garden's main focal point), is bounded on the west side, opposite the house, by a trout-filled stream that once powered the ancient mill, today no longer working but still – six centuries later – a feature of the place. A kitchen garden near the stream, which makes its gardeners self-sufficient in vegetables and fruit, and its rich dark loam – 'the best in the village' – is the result of good husbandry through hundreds of years. The 'good spread of lawn' is separated from the kitchen garden by a pergola, from springtime bedecked with climbing plants. Among these, the first to appear is a *Clematis macropetala* intermingling its beautiful, almost Wedgewood-blue flowers with crimson honeysuckle, the forerunner to an arching blush-pink, flowering mass of *Rosa* 'Albertine', which itself makes thorny contrast with *R.* 'Zephirine Drouhin', an old, thornless Bourbon rose. Beneath the pergola, snowdrops, daffodils and other bulbs commence a succession of early summer and summer colour from lupins and delphiniums, pansies, hollyhocks, an old rose, phlox, marguerites, Japanese anemonies, mallows, rudbeckia, antirrhinums, South African daisies, and *Alchemilla mollis*, its kidney-shaped leaves providing welcome foliage interest.

On the south side lies another border, a small

The pergola border. Red hot pokers, poppies, geums, lupins, delphiniums, and Turks cap lilies grow in wild and happy accord, contributing to the overall feeling of 'repose and quiet, and freedom from the bustle of the outside world'.

Part of the north side herbaceous border (to the left of the greenhouse), which includes weigela, periwinkle (Vinca spp.), Hosta fortunei, catmint (Nepeta spp.), the Hybrid Tea 'Peace' amongst other roses, Japanese anemones, the winter to spring flowering laurustinus shrub, Viburnum tinus, and the equally popular Kerria japonica 'Pleniflora' (deciduous, spring flowering and easily propagated by summer cuttings), Dutch irises, perennial asters, phlox, lupins, and paeonies.

The solid tower and graceful spire of St. Mary's, which forms the garden's main focal point.

heather garden, a bed of herbs including mints – apple and ginger and spearmint – rosemary, thyme, marjoram, sage, chives, coriander and basil, and a small, unobtrusive greenhouse produces aubergines, peppers, tomatoes, cucumbers, and other plants destined for the kitchen plot, as well as pansies and antirrhinums for the pergola border, and shrub cuttings of escallonia, cotoneaster, potentilla and japonica.

The west wall of the vicarage is clothed with blue wistaria, a red climbing rose – 'Etoile de Hollande', and, keeping it company, a clematis 'Perle d'Azur'. In the centre there is a 'Ville de Lyons' and a third clematis in the south corner, the blue-flowering 'Bee's Jubilee', a modern copy and hardier than the traditional 'Nellie Moser'.

Among the garden trees, on the north side is an ancient beech – the only tree of note in the village, a glory in autumn and host to countless starlings, for some people less welcome guests, perhaps, than the swallows who occupy the stables, the robin that has nested in the family caravan, the tree-creepers, and fly-catchers who repeatedly dive down to catch their insect food before returning to a favourite perch, or the herons or the kingfisher, who has made its nest up-stream.

This is not a plantsman's garden of carefully handpicked plants, but one that has grown up partly out of necessity (it helps provide for a family of six on the modest budget of a country clergyman), and partly out of a need for 'a place to relax and get away,' as Anne Lee, wife of the incumbent explains. For Tony Lee, who most days gets up as soon as it is light to do his part – 'mainly the manual work' – the garden is also an essential balance to his work as vicar of Childswickham. 'It's important that one isn't solely concerned with ideas, even though they may be important ideas concerned with the spiritual life of people in the parish. It is important for me to keep aware that I am a human being among other human beings, many of whom in this farming and market garden community do hard manual work for their living. If you occupy an ivory tower it is difficult to be part of parish life, to be with our people; I find it a very sobering act to work this plot of land.'

There has been a church here since Saxon times, but the main proportions of today's building were established in the fifteenth century. It was built entirely of local Cotswold stone, a deep cream limestone, mellowed after long exposure to a beautiful golden grey. The survival over the centuries of the unit of church, vicarage and garden, as spiritual focal

45

point of village life, finds expression in the attitude of parishioners both towards their vicar and their church. 'If the church roof blew off tomorrow and for some reason the insurance wasn't paid, it would be back on in no time,' laughs the vicar. 'Everyone would contribute whether they come regularly to church or not. There are a good many people in the village unable to articulate their feelings about the church, why its survival is important to them, but they feel that it is an important symbol even if the need to share in public worship isn't there. I can see this; I can feel this in people.'

As if to illustrate the support which is there in the community and has been for centuries, conversation turns to their arrival in the village in 1972. 'The previous incumbent's hobby was pheasants, peacocks and all manner of rare game birds,' Anne recalls, 'The pergola (the predecessor of the one we have now) was smothered with roses, unpruned in the ten years he had been here, and beyond it he had erected a series of wire runs – cages for his birds, over which had grown a mass of tangled ivy, elder and other weeds.' Tony was offered the cages when he came to look over the vicarage, but declined: 'He was quite a character. He had a fantastic collection of furniture, some of it obviously very valuable, inherited from his family in Yorkshire. Being a bachelor and about to retire to a small flat he reluctantly announced that he would sell off both furniture and cages in a huge auction held in the vicarage. So he dismantled the cages, rolled up the wire and did what he had to do. When we arrived to take over we saw that the cages had been erected on the truncated remains of an orchard. He had cut down these old apple and plum trees, leaving 6 feet or so of trunk, and then hung the wire over them! By the time we arrived, they were, of course, quite dead. So I enlisted the help of David Matthews, a teenager then but now one of my churchwardens, and began to dig up what was left of them. At which point Jack Simms, organist here for some fifty years and one of the local market gardeners, came up to see what was going on and said, "You need some help here," and soon returned with his tractor to which he had attached a hawser, and pulled out the roots of these old trees. When he was satisfied that we'd got out all the roots, he brought the tractor back again, this time with a Rotavator on the back (the kind they use on the fields), and gave it a good turning over.

'Later, when Jack realised I was using the kitchen garden seriously, he said, "I'll let you know when we come to plant out a particular part of the field; I'll let

Centuries of parsons who have worked the soil of this kitchen garden at Childswickham have borne witness to the words of the 19th-century gardener Canon Ellacombe, 'that such gardens are a real pleasure and refreshment to the owners, and they are none the less so when the refreshment is taken in hard manual labour.'

you know. Any plants you need, I'll bring over." And he always did – spring cabbage, cauliflowers, sprouts (this is a famous area for Brussels) – I'd find them rolled up in a newspaper on the doorstep. Sometimes he didn't ask, they'd just be left there. When he died, suddenly, two of his sons continued to run the business, and still they continue to supply us with plants.'

There are three gardeners at the vicarage at Childswickham: Tony, Anne, and Marjorie whose speciality is the greenhouse and who ten years ago came to live in the flat behind the south-side gable, the 'servants quarters' built by the Revd. Barlow in 1879. Together they have indeed created a garden 'suggestive of repose and quiet, pleasant shade, and freedom from the bustle of the outside world', and like the great clergyman gardeners before them, they have helped preserve something at the very core of English village life.

THE GARDEN AT
Grantchester

Mr. and Mrs. Jeffrey Archer

**'There is no wind and no sun, only a sort of warm haze,
and through it the mingled country sounds of a bee, a
mowing machine, a mill and a sparrow. Peace!'**

Rupert Brooke

*View of the Old Vicarage across the herbaceous border, taken
from beneath a high yet fairly dense canopy of yew where,
surprisingly, old species roses manage to grow alongside
colourful nasturtiums, heathers, potentilla and the horizontal
spreading branches and white flower clusters of Viburnum
tomentosum 'Plicatum'.*

For most of us, the Old Vicarage garden at Grant-chester is the quintessential English vicarage garden. That this is so is due of course to Rupert Brooke's poem, 'The Old Vicarage, Grantchester' and the nostalgia for England's green and pleasant land, which it so successfully evokes. The nostalgia derives from the fact that Brooke wrote the poem from afar, in the Café des Westens, Berlin, while he watched 'Temperamentvoll German Jews/Drink beer around . . .' Originally the poem was entitled 'Home' and when first published, in the June 1912 issue of the King's College undergraduate magazine, *Basileon*, it appeared under the title, 'Fragments of a Poem to be entitled The Sentimental Exile'. Brooke was missing home, and in particular he was remembering the idyllic summer he had spent a year earlier, in 1911, in the Old Vicarage.

As a young undergraduate at King's College,

Cambridge, he had admired both house and garden from The Orchard, the house next door, where he had rooms. And in December 1910, having complained to his mother that 'horrible people' had appeared at The Orchard, he moved there with his books and belongings. His new landlord, Mr. Neeve, kept bees, and, as Brooke wrote in a letter to Lytton Strachey, 'The Neeves are "working people" who have "taken the house and want lodgers". Mr. Neeve is a refined creature, with an accent above his class, who sits out near the beehives with a handkerchief over his head and reads advanced newspapers. He knows a lot about botany. They keep babies and chickens: and I rather think I have seen both classes entering the house. But you could be firm. The garden is the great glory. There is a soft lawn with a sundial, and tangled, antique flowers abundantly; and a sham ruin, quite in a corner, built about 50 years ago by a historian and rector of Grantchester. He used to feast there nightly with . . . I don't know whom. But they still do, spectrally, in the evenings; with faint lights and odd noises.'

Clearly Mr. Neeve's botanical knowledge was put to good use in the garden, for flowers are the first image recalled of Grantchester in Brooke's poem:

Brooke's 'tunnel of green gloom' formed by a line of chestnuts, with the river beyond.

> *Just now the lilac is in bloom,*
> *All before my little room;*
> *And in my flower-beds, I think,*
> *Smile the carnation and the pink;*
> *And down the borders, well I know,*
> *The poppy and the pansy blow . . .*
> *Oh! there the chestnuts, summer through,*
> *Beside the river make for you*
> *A tunnel of green gloom, and sleep*
> *Deeply above; and green and deep*
> *The stream mysterious glides beneath,*
> *Green as a dream and deep as death.*

Flowers in borders and woodland walks, and the 'tunnel of green gloom' formed by giant chestnuts on the bank of the river, remain much as Brooke describes. But Grantchester is not in any sense a pretty garden, anymore than it was in the poet's day. Its appeal lies in its wildness, its naturalness, the trees and shrubs which tell of its age, and the 'stream mysterious', which in its tardy, endless motion by, seems almost to mock the transience of the lives of people who have dwelt here over the centuries.

The house itself was built in about 1683, though an earlier vicarage, parts of which are included in the seventeenth-century building, appears in records dated 1380, 1440, and again in 1550. Brooke was at once absorbed by a sense of its history, writing to his cousin, Erica Cotterill, 'This is a deserted, lonely, dank, ruined, overgrown, gloomy, lovely house: with a garden to match. It is all of five hundred years old, and fusty with the ghosts of generations of mouldering clergymen. It is a fit place to write my poetry in.' And so it fell to the poet to give the vicarage's past inhabitants the immortality that Nature denied them:

> *And in that Garden, black and white,*
> *Creep whispers through the grass all night;*
> *And spectral dance, before the dawn,*
> *A hundred Vicars down the lawn;*
> *Curates, long dust, will come and go*
> *On lissom, clerical, printless toe;*
> *And oft between the boughs is seen*
> *The sly shade of a Rural Dean.*

So strongly did he feel about the continuance of the old vicarage that in 1914 when he heard of plans to demolish it, Brooke, by then a sub-lieutenant in the RNVR, rattled off a letter to Frances Cornford asking her 'to find out if that's so; by whose orders; and what steps could be taken in the way of saving it. I

The sundial, 1862. The stone book reads: 'From the rising of the Sun until the going down of the same the Lord's name is to be praised.' It stands on a pedestal made from one of the old crosses from the church chancel.

The sham ruin or 'falling house that never falls'. Brooke was wrong, it was built not by a clergyman but by Samuel Widnall, a sometime market gardener, who, nevertheless, is said to have affected the appearance of a cleric.

mean could one buy it, or the land. It seems to me very important.'

Fortunately, he had been misinformed, and today the vicarage is the home of Mr. Jeffrey Archer, a novelist and playwright, his wife Mary, a chemist and Fellow of Newnham College, and their two sons. With help of a full-time gardener they have produced a fine garden and preserved its famous aspects, including Brooke's 'falling house that never falls' (which in fact did fall but was subsequently re-built and now, rather oddly, carries a road sign for Louth, where Mr. Archer was Member of Parliament from 1969). The garden is open to the public through the National Gardens Scheme.

It is extraordinary how the memory of these lovely old vicarage gardens lingers on in one's mind, and for Rupert Brooke his experience of Grantchester during the warm summer of 1911 was a rare moment of true happiness – 'There is no wind and no sun, only a sort of warm haze,' he wrote to Ka Cox, 'and

through it the mingled country sounds of a bee, a mowing machine, a mill and a sparrow. Peace!' Homesick in Berlin, the image must have been doubly strong – 'I've a fancy you may be, just now, in Grantchester. That river and the chestnuts come back to me a lot . . .

> *Say, do the elm-clumps greatly stand,*
> *Still guardians of that holy land?*
> *The chestnuts shade, in reverend dream,*
> *The yet unacademic stream?*
> *Is dawn a secret shy and cold*
> *Anadyomene, silver-gold?*
> *And sunset still a golden sea*
> *From Haslingfield to Madingley?*
> *And after, ere the night is born,*
> *Do hares come out about the corn?*
> *Oh, is the water sweet and cool*
> *Gentle and brown, above the pool?*
> *And laughs the immortal river still*
> *Under the mill, under the mill?*
> *Say, is there Beauty yet to find?*
> *And certainty? and Quiet kind?*
> *Deep meadows yet, for to forget*
> *The lies, and truths, and pain? . . . oh! yet*
> *Stands the Church clock at ten to three?*
> *And is there honey still for tea?*

By the first week of July 1912, Brooke was back at the Old Vicarage in person. 'You see?' said Mrs. Neeve, bringing in the tea-tray on his first afternoon home, 'There *is* honey still for tea.'

THE GARDEN AT
Eversley

The Reverend Canon Charles Kingsley

'When I walk the fields I am oppressed every now and
then with an innate feeling, that everything I see has a
meaning, if I could understand it . . . Everything seems to
be full of God's reflex, if we could but see it.'

Charles Kingsley, popularly known as the author of *The Water Babies*, arrived at Eversley in
Hampshire in 1842 at the age of 23, and spent the first six weeks of his life as rector's curate lodging
in the rectory house. Shortly after his arrival, he sent a sketch of the view from Eversley Rectory, to
Frances, the woman who was eighteen months later to become his wife: 'Can you understand my
sketch? I am no drawer of trees, but the view is beautiful. The ground slopes upward from the
windows to a sunk fence and road, without banks or hedges, and then rises in the furze hill in the
drawing, which hill is perfectly beautiful in light and shade, and colour . . . Behind the acacia on
the lawn you get the first glimpse of the fir-forests and moors, of which the five-sixths of my parish

Kingsley walking up the lane in front of the rectory.

consist. Those delicious self-sown firs! Every step I wander they whisper to me of you, the delicious past melting into the more delicious future.'

In almost daily letters he describes the beauty of the surrounding countryside: 'It is hotter than yesterday, if possible, so I wandered out into the fields, and have been passing the morning in a lonely woodland bath – a little stream that trickles off the moor – with the hum of bees, and the sleepy song of birds around me, and the feeling of the density of life in myriads of insects and flowers strong upon me, drinking in all the forms of beauty which lie in the leaves and pebbles, and mossy nooks of damp tree roots, and all the lowly intricacies of nature which no one stoops to see.'

The young clergyman's faith is constantly re-affirmed by the forms and patterns of Nature which he divines as he walks about his country parish, and he writes of 'the belief which is becoming every day stronger with me that all symmetrical natural objects, aye, and perhaps all forms, colours, and scents which show organisation or arrangement, are types of some spiritual truth or existence, of a grade between the symbolical type and the mystic type.'

So successful was Charles Kingsley's short curacy that after the rector's death, and a voluble campaign undertaken by the villagers themselves, he was recalled to become Eversley's new rector.

Kingsley's love of Nature was both the fount of his faith and the reason why he was so loved. His parishioners were people whose lives moved in sympathy with the rhythms of God's creation; they sustained their lives from the soil, and, as Frances Kingsley recalls, were steeped in rural traditions and

a morality at odds with a fast-changing, modern world. Life in Eversley was immutable: 'Every man in those days could snare his hare, and catch a good dinner of fish in waters not then strictly preserved; and the old women would tell of the handsome muffs and tippets, made of pheasants' feathers, not bought with silver, which they wore in their young days.' Kingsley's secret was that 'he could swing a flail with the threshers in the barn, turn his swathe with the mowers in the meadow, pitch hay with the hay-

Charles Kingsley was not the only gardener in the family. His cousin, William, who was incumbent of South Kilvington in Yorkshire for 57 years and died in harness aged 101, appended a message to the gate of his garden (shown here) which read, 'Trespassers beware! Polypodiums and Scolopendriums set in these grounds.'

makers in the pasture. From knowing every fox earth on the moor, the "ready hover" of the pike, the still hole where the chub lay, he had always a word in sympathy for the huntsman or the old poacher. With the farmer he discussed the rotation of the crops, and with the labourer the science of hedging and ditching. And yet while he seemed to ask for information, he unconsciously gave more than he received.'

Upon the Kingsleys' arrival at Eversley in 1844 there was much to be done. Not only did the garden slope upwards away from the rectory, as Charles had earlier described, but these natural draining problems were compounded by a line of fish ponds running from the glebe field, past the house, and joining a large pond belonging to the Church Farm, behind the church itself. 'The house was damp and unwholesome,' recalled Frances, 'surrounded with ponds which overflowed with every heavy rain, and flooded not only the garden and stables, but all the rooms on the ground floor, keeping up master and servants sometimes all night, baling out the water in buckets for hours together; and drainage works had to be done before it was habitable.'

Kingsley's daughter, Rose, takes up the story, in an excerpt from her book, *Eversley Gardens and Others*: 'He at once became his own engineer and gardener. The ponds, except three in the glebe field which in course of time were stocked with trout, were drained. 'Against the south wall of the house which looks

on the dear "Study Garden", a Magnolia, *M. grandiflora*, was trained, filling the air and all the rooms with its fragrance. It still lives; and has, I hope, lately taken a new lease of life: but having for some years been used by rats as a ladder to the window of an upper room, it was in a sad state six years ago; and only the utmost care has saved it from utter destruction. *Lonicera flexuosa, Clematis montana, Wistaria*, "Gloire de Dijon" and "Ayrshire" Roses, with a fine variegated Ivy, hid the wall in a veil of verdure and sweetness. The great treasure of the Study Garden was – alas! it is no more – an immense plant of the Japanese Honeysuckle, *L. japonica* "Aureoreticulata", trained over an iron umbrella in front of the study window.

'Next to the Golden Honeysuckle the pride of the Study Garden lay in its Yellow Persian Briar-roses. These, which came originally from the great plant in the corner of the troco ground at Bramshill, grew very freely; and in June the walls of the house and garden were ablaze with the vivid golden blossoms, the rooms being always decorated for two or three weeks with dishes of the yellow Roses, mixed with darkest

'The Study Garden, up and down which my father paced bare-headed, composing sermon or novel, lecture or poem; for he never indulged in rough copy, every sentence being thought out first, and then written or dictated straight off with hardly a correction.'

purple Pansies on a ground of wild Fern.' Later, Rose recalls how the low-lying rectory garden's vulnerability to early and late frosts, together with the lightness of its soil, has meant that 'none but the hardiest and

The Study Garden, 1865, shows Kingsley with his younger son, Grenville, for whom 'The Water Babies' was written.

most common plants could be grown out of doors. Yet despite these drawbacks the borders were always as bright as those in more favoured spots, filled with such plants as Phloxes, Delphiniums, Alyssums, Saxifrages, Pinks, Pansies, and, above all, Roses and Carnations which grew in profusion without the least trouble. And perhaps the gayest moment of the Rectory garden, was when every border round the house was edged with a thick band of blue Forget-me-not outside another of pink Silene, so that the old mellow brick walls rose from out of a lovely setting of pale blue and pink. One bay on the front of the house was well covered with Pyracantha, in which a pair of white-throats built for many years undisturbed, just under my mother's window. The farther bay, up to 1860-1, was quite covered by a magnificent plant of the Noisette Rose, "Jaune Desprez": but the severe cold of that Winter killed it to our lasting sorrow, for it had been our pride and glory, and its place was taken by hardy creepers. Over the glass porch of the front door *Clematis jackmanni*, the white cluster Rose "Felicité Perpétue" and *Chaenomeles japonica* were woven in lovely confusion. The chaenomeles still exists; and its scarlet flowers still go, as in old days, to help to decorate the church at Easter.

'Rhododendrons loved the peat that could be had for the carting from the bogs just beyond the Mount. They grew luxuriantly; and the neighbours always came to see the Rector's garden when the big beds on either side of the front gate were in blossom. At the end of the Study Garden, between these beds and the stable-yard, was a little Rose garden, a choice and sheltered retreat, with a pink Thorn in one corner near the gate, and pillar Roses at the back of the border. And in one of the big bushes that shut it off from the drive a black-cap built year after year, to my father's extreme delight, so tame that we could watch his little throat as the enchanting notes of his song rose in the air. I specially remember among those pillar Roses in my childhood, "Chenédolé", "Fulgens", "Gloire des Rosomanes", "Fellenberg", "Aimée Vibert", "Coupe d'Hébé", crimson "Madame Desprez", and "Maria Leonida".

For the Kingsley children, Eversley was a paradise. The back garden was given over to their own little plots, and Rose managed to get an extra portion containing a fine standard of 'Coupe d'Hébé'. 'But after hours spent in sowing and raking, great was the fall of my pride when George Chaplin remarked as he passed, "Why, Miss Rose, have the hens been a-scratching here?"'

Their father built them a hut for an outdoor nursery in a real bit of primaeval forest at the end of a walk that led from the rectory's stable-yard. This was

View across the back garden near where the Kingsley children had their plots.

the 'furze hill' that their father had described in that first letter to Frances in 1842. Known as the Mount, and crowned with an ancient pollard oak, this spot had become in the course of time one of Charles Kingsley's favourite spots – 'covered with fine oaks and hollies, beeches, wild cherries, and crab trees – the ground below white in Spring-time with wood anemones, blue with wild hyacinths, and jewelled with primroses and meadow orchis; while on the open slope beneath the great oak, the wild thyme in summer grows in thick, fragrant cushions. The old hollow oak, which according to the best authorities must have been a lusty young tree at the time of the Norman Conquest, became a favourite resort of us children; for by means of two or three stout bars across the rent in its side we could climb into its enormous branches, and there read, or attempt to learn our lessons. But it was not a place for very concentrated study, as birds and beetles, squirrels and butterflies, were most engaging and distracting neighbours.'

'Strangely diversified were the visitors who found their way to the Rectory in those days. One Sunday, I seem to see a tired compositor from a great London printing-house, who had come down to talk over the grievances of his fellow-workmen. Another Sunday, that Royal personage whom my father loved with

The summer house on the Mount, 1860.

The furze hill or Mount, as it was known, opposite the rectory.
Right, a Wellingtonia, grown from one of two seeds in a cone Kingsley picked up in May, 1874.

such devoted loyalty, sitting on his fine brown charger at the door, before riding back to the camp of his gallant 10th Hussars in Bramshill Park. Yet again, gentle Queen Emma of the Sandwich Islands, coming to stay with the man whose books she and her husband had read in their far-off Pacific kingdom, and to see what English boys' cricket was like at Wellington College. Or Alfred Tennyson – as he then was – smoking pipes in the study, when he came to see whether the beautiful old Brick House Farm, close to the Mount, would be a fit place to settle in when he won his lovely bride.

'But more precious by far are memories of the quiet home life. Hot days when my father would tempt his favourite pair of natterjacks [running toads] from their hole in the lawn beyond the Acacia tree, and walk up and down admiring the colours on their backs, while the little creatures sat contentedly in his hand; or when he would persuade the

An avenue of Irish yews planted by Kingsley in the churchyard, part of a scheme intended to provide his parishioners with beautiful objects to look upon as they assembled in the churchyard 'for their Sunday gossip before service'. In 1862, Kingsley's pupil John Martineau, came upon the couple busily planting shrubs, and climbing roses for the church's brick walls. 'It will be the prettiest churchyard that ever was seen,' he wrote.

The produce of the other seed from Kingsley's cone potted by Rose, and then planted in Eversley churchyard.

square stone still marks the grave of the beloved Dandy Dinmont, my father's devoted companion and friend; the inscription he wrote still fresh upon it:

"DANDY, 1849-61. *Fideli Fideles.*"

While but a few yards away, close to the garden he made, in the churchyard he planted, shaded by the Fir trees he loved – a living presence still to those who knew him, helper and comforter still to thousands who never saw his face, faithful to the end to his Church, to his ideals, to his fellow-man, Dandy's master rests.'

The Kingsleys' grave, shaded by three giant, 17th-century firs that grow in the rectory garden just beyond the wall.

half-tame slow-worm to come out of his nest in the steep, Thyme-grown bank of the sunk fence. Memories of warm Summer evenings, when, in the soft dusk, German part songs and English glees would float up in the still air beneath the huge canopy of the Fir boughs; and my father would ask for one and another of his favourites, or bid the singers listen to the chirring of the nightjar, or hold up a hand to point out the stealthy flight of a white barn-owl.'

Frances recalls two other little friends he had in a pair of sand wasps, 'who lived in a crack of the window in his dressing-room, one of which he had saved from drowning in a hand-basin, taking it tenderly out into the sunshine to dry; and every spring he would look out eagerly for them or their children who came out of, or returned to, the same crack.'

'The natterjacks have gone', Rose continues. 'So has the slow-worm. Black and tabby cats have taken the place of the white ones that peopled the stables.

'But in the garden under the Fir trees, a little

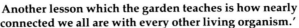

Another lesson which the garden teaches is how nearly connected we all are with every other living organism.'

Henry Nicholson Ellacombe

Bulwick Rectory is the home of the Rural Theology Association which was begun by Mervyn Wilson because he felt that the Church has 'lost sight of the Bible teaching on the great theme of Creation. Since the coming of the Industrial Revolution, the attention of our society has become more and more centred on matters affecting urban and suburban Britain. The Church as an institution has largely followed the assumptions of secular society and concentrated its resources and directed much of its paid manpower to urban and suburban areas.' Ironically it was not in the rural surroundings of Bulwick, near Corby in Northamptonshire, that Mervyn first realised the importance of being in touch with nature but while he was Rector of Bermondsey. 'Allotments were started on the Surrey Docks soon after they were filled in and before development took place. It was most interesting to see the effect on the character of those who took them up. These people lived in flats without any space. I remember one man in particular, his temper was improved no end! He had been a very reserved man and I suspect a bit crotchety at times when he got home. He became a changed man, so great was the satisfaction in getting down and working the soil, even though the soil itself was virtually dead – it had been underwater for so long – no life, distinctly grey, almost eerie.'

Bulwick Rectory consists of some 6 acres, a small-holding in a manorial estate, the Tryon Estate, owned by the Conant family, who have been its proprietors since 1660. Nearby Harringworth, which with Laxton and Bulwick comprises the rector's parish responsibility, also used to be owned by the Conants but has been gradually sold off and now largely converted into a commuter town replete with executive bungalows and all modern conveniences. Bulwick however, is very definitely not for sale, and one has the impression that the Conants are quite fussy about whom they permit to live on their property. As a result the way of life of its people has been relatively unaffected by modern trends.

The rector, his wife and six children share their acreage with two horses, five ewes, two rams, six lambs, numerous geese, hens (which at certain times have free rein in the garden), a very handsome cock, and a collection of bee hives. In their first year the Wilsons also had to keep cattle, but found them

tricky – 'if you're not 100% sure what you are doing they are all too easy to lose.' Then they tried bottle-fed lambs for two or three years, but they turned out to be constant work, so they progressed to ewes. The secret of their success with these lies in help freely offered by a churchwarden who is a sheep farmer and assists them with the numerous injections, nail parings, sheerings, and dippings that they require.

Having all the animals provides a common point of interest and conversation with Mervyn Wilson's parishioners. 'You must have a country interest if you live around here,' he says, and gives an example of how their lives connect with those of their parishioners on a daily basis: 'Last night the treasurer of one of our parishes rang up and asked whether we'd like to put one of our hives of bees in his bean field which is just coming into flower.'

'And there's the village barter system,' continues Mrs. Wilson. 'The other day I looked in on the farmer

The boundary – a hedge of hornbeam – between Folly Garden and Daffodil Walk.

who put the nitrogen on our hayfield back in March and said that I hadn't had a bill from him, so he thought for a bit – he couldn't remember how much he'd put on – and then said, "Oh, give me some honey instead."'

The rectory fields are left to the sheep, horses, and children, and the garden, roughly 1 acre, is divided up into a number of plots, each of which has its special use or character. 'The main principle of any working garden must be to keep things as much as possible in their proper place. When we came to Bulwick the garden was just one big open field. We have divided it into a nursery garden, a vegetable garden, a folly garden, a daffodil walk, and a medlar garden. The Victorians realised the importance of creating favourable mini-environments for their plants, and planted lots of shrubberies and box hedges to harbour them. I have done the same, using yew and hornbeam hedges, wire fencing and the boundary walls that already existed. These separate

The rector, his wife and six children share the garden with 2 horses, 5 ewes, 2 rams, 6 lambs, a very handsome cock and a number of hens and geese.

one garden from another and help to keep marauders out!

'The second main principle concerns paths. If you are using a garden all the time, summer and winter, you must have hard paths otherwise the barrows get stuck and animals and humans ensure that the place becomes a mess.'

In the nursery, on the garden's south side, young plants are brought on – we saw scorzonera, a walnut tree growing from a nut, apples growing from pips and another apple – grafted, seedling conifers (pine, yew and holly to supplement the hedges), poppies, and plum trees.

A large kitchen garden on the north boundary contains a wide variety of vegetables, fruit and nuts. 'We're a family of eight,' says Mrs. Wilson, 'and only buy food very occasionally. We grow everything you might expect plus various unusual early spring sprouting things: the scorzonera is grown for its spring greens as much as its root, and there's seakael, a great Victorian favourite, land cress and chives and sorrel. You can achieve a very satisfactory and quite substantial salad in April and early May when there's very little else.

'Fruit trees have strayed into the flower garden simply because we like to grow so much fruit and prefer fruit trees to cordons because they are more abundant and resistant to disease. And some flowers

Papaver orientale, grown from seed in the nursery garden.

The church from the front garden at Bulwick Rectory, where Mervyn Wilson expounds the theology of God the Creator: 'It is the contribution of the rural theologian to speak of the natural world as he finds it.' His garden is open to the public on certain days each year.

have strayed into the vegetable garden where the site is better for them – the alstroemeria do so well under the kitchen garden wall, undisturbed among the fruit trees, spinach and so on.'

Next to the nursery lies the folly garden, so named because of a new folly built to match an ancient dovecot near the kitchen garden, a relic of the days when the rector kept pigeons and ate the breasts of young fledglings before they learned to fly. Mervyn Wilson assures us that he is not tempted to re-establish the tradition, 'though we do fatten cockerels there in the autumn'. Planted among apple trees are old shrub roses, lupins, delphiniums, paeonies, *Salvia pretensis* and red hot pokers (*Kniphofia spp.*) – a real cottage garden. On this June day the colour effects of a red paeony and self-sown columbine (*Aquilegia spp.*) and a purple geranium growing

Part of the Medlar Garden where the rector grows a variety of shrubs and herbaceous plants in addition to a medlar and quince, so popular among Victorian gardeners.

freely among the variegated foliage of a dogwood (*Cornus spp.*), are especially striking.

The northern boundary of the folly garden, a hedge of hornbeam, conceals the daffodil walk, a vista looking down to an old gnarled mulberry tree and the house. When the daffodils have finished, the grass on each edge of the 'tunnel' is left to grow until early July when it is cut to produce a wholly different spatial effect.

West from the folly, and nearer the house, we come to the medlar garden. The medlar itself was very popular with the Victorians, as was the quince, also grown here. Among the flowers, a yellow potentilla, martagon lilies, a daphne, already smelling good, more paeonies, a big sterile blackberry bush (*Rubus* 'Tridel'), and beneath it an elaeagnus.

Here amongst his animals, plants and produce, the Wilsons practise the first principle of the Theology of Creation, what he calls the primary production cycle.

Be fruitful and multiply; fill the earth and subdue it, rule over the fish in the sea, the birds of heaven, and every living thing that moves upon the earth. Genesis

'Only the primary producer actually knows what it means to tend and rule and subdue with his own hands. These things remain book learning for the townsman, bright ideas untarnished, unenriched by the necessity to kill as well as to bring to birth.

'The fruit farmer kills the aphis and the larva of the codling moth. The gardener does his best to destroy the hosts of the scale insects and the potato boring wireworm and the leaf killing red spider. Thorn hedges are cut and laid to keep in livestock. Trees are felled for the carpenter and for firewood. The ground is scarred for building materials. The gardener plants two shrubs close together; one he must uproot if the other is to thrive.

'Many town and suburban dwellers do reflect on

The Folly Garden: Russell lupins grown from seed the previous year, white thalictrum — self-sown, and Phlomis viscosa. Delphiniums and shrub roses in the background.

these things. Their difficulty is lack of first-hand knowledge, and thorough realistic analysis. (Very few country people become sentimental vegetarians.) The problem for the city dweller is that the only form of life he really knows is human. So it is the contribution of the rural theologian to speak of the natural world as he finds it, alive with its own life, and playing its own part in the vastly complicated inter-relationship of this cosmic order.

'Here at Bulwick all kitchen waste goes to the geese, hens or compost; compost and manure fertilise the garden; the garden produces vegetables and fruit that last all year, and so the cycle continues. Man consumes and he works; that's his place in the cycle. If you think that food simply comes out of a shop or a freezer then you are denying a relationship with the natural world and unable to appreciate where you are, what Man's purpose is in God's world.'

The rector's beehives and, behind the yew, the dovecot.

Wider shot of the Folly Garden where besides such herbaceous plants as have already been mentioned, the rector grows 3 apple trees, a number of shrubs and 20 different roses.

Selective Plant Lists

Trees and shrubs in the Medlar	*Old Roses in the Folly*
Medlar	'Maigold'
Quince	'Golden Wings'
Acer griseum	'Queen of Denmark'
Viburnum davidii	'Mme. Plantier'
V. 'Burkwoodii'	'The Reeve'
V. plicatum tomentosum	'Canary Bird'
Cotoneaster salicifolius	'Proud Titania'
C. lactifolius	'Lordly Oberon'
Deutzia 'Elegantissimus'	'Charles de Mills'
D. 'Kalmiiflora'	'Francesca'
Coronilla emerus	'Blush Damask'
Cornus kousa	'Penelope'
Kolkwitzia amabilis	*pimpinellifolia*
Rubus 'Tridel'	*rugosa*
Elaeagnus pungens 'Maculata'	'Comaeieux'
E. multiflora	'Mundi'
E. 'Ebbingei'	'Mme. Hardy'
Philadelphus	'Tour de Malakoff'
Lonicera 'Purpusii'	'Cornelia'
Cotinus coggygria	'Celsiana'
Daphne 'Burkwoodii'	'Honorine de Brabant'
Potentilla	'Paulii'
Euonymus	*moyesii*

Rectory, c. 1820, and in flower Viburnum opulus, the guelder rose, grown from seed, and Robinia pseudoacacia 'Frisia' just coming into leaf. Below, the Nursery Garden.

Selborne

The Reverend Gilbert White

'We have met him in the woods and in the fields, in the village, in his study with a book or a pen in his hand. At last we find him in his garden!'

Samuel Reynolds Hole

Gilbert White is without doubt the most famous clergyman naturalist of all time and his book, *The Natural History and Antiquities of Selborne*, first published in 1789 and since then re-issued in more than 150 new editions and impressions, is almost certainly the world's most widely read book on natural history.

Much of his precise observation of the wild life of this tiny Hampshire village, which forms the substance of the book and which White delivered in the form of letters, took place in the 7-acre garden behind his house. There he constructed two alcoves connected with the house by a long brick path so that he could reach them come rain, come shine. The second of these alcoves, the one farthest from the house, was a simple arbour set among 20-foot field hedges of beech and thorn, an ideal environment for birds and naturalist to get to know one another.

Selborne itself provides an extraordinary diversity of soil and aspect, which perhaps explains why it attracts so rich a variety of natural life. 'The parish of Selborne,' Gilbert White explained, 'lies in the extreme eastern corner of the county of Hampshire, bordering on the county of Sussex, and not far from the county of Surrey . . . The high part of the south-west consists of a vast hill of chalk, rising 300 feet above the village, and is divided into a sheep-down, the high wood and a long hanging wood, called The Hanger. The covert of this eminence is altogether beech . . . The prospect is bounded to the south-east and east by the vast range of mountains called the Sussex Downs . . . The village consists of one single, straggling street, three-quarters of a mile in length, in a sheltered vale, and running parallel with the hanger . . .

'The cart-way of the village divides, in a remarkable way, two very incongruous soils. To the south-west is rank clay, that requires the labour of years to render it mellow; while the gardens to the north-east . . . consist of a warm, forward, crumbling mould, called black malm, which seems highly saturated with vegetable and animal manure.'

So remote was this strip of a village in White's time, and so poorly served by its 'hollow lanes', that in winter it would be completely cut off for months at a time – either choked by snow-drifts or made unapproachable by floods or mud. Even in summer, access was not guaranteed unless you happen to have had your carriage or cart wheels made by the local wheelwright, who ensured that all conveyances conformed to the guage of the deep tracks of its narrow lanes.

Gilbert White was born in the vicarage at Selborne in 1720, when his grandfather (also named Gilbert White) was the vicar. Soon afterwards he left the county in his parents care, who sojourned in Surrey and Sussex until Gilbert was about 10 years old. Then, following his grandfather's death, he and his family returned to Selborne and, with Gilbert's grandmother, took up residence in The Wakes, the name of the house which, except for a short period at Oxford University, was to be Gilbert's home for the next sixty-three years. The Wakes was in fact owned by Gilbert's uncle, who was Rector of nearby Swarraton and who was later to provide the young cleric with one of his many curacies.

It is not at all clear how much forward thinking went into young Gilbert's future, but once he became an undergraduate at Oriel he effectively discounted himself as a future vicar of Selborne, for Selborne was a living solely in the gift of Magdalene College. Perhaps, at this time, he had in mind an academic career, for in due course he became a Fellow of Oriel. But if he did, it didn't last. Richard Mabey, in his recent biography of White, portrays him as quite a worldly figure and convivial Fellow, a clergyman who enjoyed good living and with an eye for *a* good living provided residence wasn't essential.

The original house dates back to the 16th century. White would have known the right-hand portion.

Eschewing an academic career, White returned to the Wakes and followed 'the accepted and acceptable privilege that followed upon taking orders', namely pluralism. The approbation comes from H.J. Massingham's *The Writings of Gilbert White of Selborne*. At one time or another, and very often at the same time, White served curacies at Swarraton, Durley, West Dene, Farringdon, Newton Valence, Selborne (on four occasions), and even managed one at Moreton Pinckney in Northamptonshire. As with any privilege, the practice of pluralism was open to exploitation – how much did (or could) the curate serve his many parishes, and how much did the curacy serve him? For instance, one cannot help wondering how often White made the long and difficult journey to care for his flock at Moreton Pinckney, particularly as he was known to suffer from coach sickness.

The curacies made White comfortably off compared to the working man, but he wasn't as rich as the landed gentry, and what we know of his garden makes it plain that he maintained a necessarily, perhaps characteristically frugal nature. For example, in imitation of William Kent, the famous landscape gardener who proposed that urns, obelisks and statues be placed in a romantic, natural setting, White erected two ornamental jar vases in the garden of The Wakes, one on a pedestal 9 feet high. But the pedestal was made of wood not stone, and the vases were second-hand containers used earlier, perhaps, for olive oil. Again, he erected a 12-foot high statue of Hercules, carefully working out the perspective so that it was clearly visible through six different gates in his hedges. But it wasn't a proper statue; it was a picture of Hercules painted on a board so as to look like one.

The only remaining portion of the 'hollow lane', which in White's day was the sole link with the outside world.

Once Gilbert White had left Oxford and committed himself to living at The Wakes, he threw himself wholeheartedly into his 7-acre garden. Ample evidence of this lies in the *Garden Kalendar*, a regular record of events which he kept over a twenty-year period from 1751. From the *Garden Kalendar* it is clear that White was his own gardener. In an introduction to a numbered edition of White's works, Dean Hole records: 'He believed that the golden rule, which prevailed in his day as a condition of success in agriculture, that

> *"He who by his plough would thrive,*
> *Himself must either hold or drive,"*

was to be observed in horticulture, and that no man will work quite so well for another as he can work for

himself . . . His nephews "John" and "Tull" were his subordinates. He employs labourers two or three at a time to do rough work; "Dame Turner and her girls" come in to weed the walks; but he sows his own choice seed, strikes his own cuttings, prunes his vines, transplants a mulberry tree which he had raised from a layer, makes a bed of aromatic herbs, superintends the grubbing, burning, and planting in new ground added to his garden, the cutting of the alleys, the levelling of his terrace . . .'

It is helpful to think of White's garden as being divided into two parts: an inner garden (itself composed of a number of individual gardens) and the outer fields, where once White's 20-foot high hedges grew. The majestic 'hanging wood' of beech trees, which today extends to cover the 'pleasing park-like spot' that White described as existing south-east of his garden, still forms its splendid south-west boundary, and the house, with its Victorian and Edwardian additions to the cottage White knew, dominates its north-eastern side. The two parts of the garden – inner and outer – reflected the two styles of gardening which White pursued, the traditional kitchen-come-flower, 'plantsman' style and the then increasingly popular landscape style, respectively.

In the outer garden White already had the 'romantic and natural setting' that Kent had proposed, so there was no real need to sculpt the land, though he did form a small mound (about 6 feet high and 9 feet in diameter) at the bottom of 'the great Mead' (meadow), and Hercules of course stood somewhere near the base of The Hanger, at the culmination of a

Plan of the Inner Garden

1 White's orchard
2 Yew Tree
3 Lime tree
4 Route to Turner's Garden
5 Field Garden & melonry
6 White's ha-ha and sundial separating
  inner and outer gardens
7 The laburnum arch
8 White's fruit wall
9 Rose Garden
10 Annual Garden
11 Herb Garden
12 Water Garden

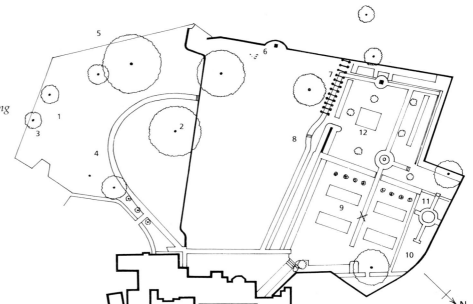

The Field Garden where White had his melonry. The Hanger in the background.

vista of carefully positioned gates in his tall hedges.

Walking due south from the house past the brick path that led to his observatories, we approach the original site of his orchard and shrubbery. To our right grows an enormous yew, which White almost certainly knew, and in our path is a lime tree, a direct descendant of the trees White himself planted in front of the local butcher's shop to hide the 'blood and filth' in the unfortunate trader's windows. Suckers from a huge wych elm (the spot which its enormous bole occupied still clearly visible) sustain further a connection with the garden's past as do spring flowering wild tulips (*Tulipa sylvestris*) which, with lilies, hollyhocks, wallflowers and columbines, once grew amongst his filbert, apple, plum and pear trees, and his Dutch medlar and cherries that completed his orchard.

Further up Baker's hill, and separated by a quick-set hedge, was Turner's Garden (presumably adjacent to Turner's Cottage from which Dame Turner and her girls would have come to help with the weeding). Turner's Garden was a vegetable plot containing beans, cabbages, celery, carrots, radishes, turnips, leeks and cucumbers. Farther on, White arranged fir trees into a quincunx (one at each corner of a rectangle and one in the middle); and nearby he erected one of his ornamental oil jars.

Then, as we turn south-west towards The Hanger, we come to the field garden and White's melonry.

Wild tulips, Tulipa sylvestris, growing on Baker's Hill, as they did in Gilbert White's day.

The cantaloupe melon, an obsession for White.

White had a 'thing' about the Cantaloupe melon: 'It was a speciality with Gilbert White,' records Dean Hole, 'not so much as being of all the melons the most palatable, but chiefly because its successful culture was a chief ambition among gardeners, and required all their care and skill. On his return from Oxford or from visits to friends, he hastens to inspect his beds of Cantaloupes, as a young mother rushes to the nursery after absence, or a schoolboy home for the holidays to his pony in the stable.' David

The Annual Garden, where David Standing has planted a profusion of flowers that Gilbert White knew: aster, sweet pea, candytuft, love-in-the-mist, balsam, love-lies-bleeding (G.W. called it 'the pendulous amaranth') and marigolds.

Standing, who is today in charge of the garden at The Wakes and is in the process of restoring its plants to those White knew, has plans to re-make the melonry, small-scale, 'I counted that out of the 220 pages of the *Garden Kalendar*, 163 carry mention of his melons, so it was obviously an absolute mania with him.'

White grew his melons on hot beds of fresh manure with a shallow covering of soil, and includes in the *Kalendar* a long list of the farmers from whom he acquired it. On April 3rd, 1759, we hear from White that because 'the Cantaloupe bed [is] not coming to a proper degree of Heat, I ordered it to be pulled to pieces, & worked-up with ten loads of fresh hot dung just brought in. The labourers made-use of about sixteen loads of the first bed again: the new bed contains twenty-six loads. Laid some loam all over to keep-down the steam . . .'

'In fact,' continues David Standing, 'Gilbert White followed Philip Miller's instructions very closely, for example his melonry faces roughly south-east. Philip Miller ran the Chelsea Physic Garden in London [the world's second oldest botanical garden] and made it famous all over Europe; he was one of the most famous eighteenth-century gardeners. If you look at his *Garden Dictionary* you can compare – sometimes

What remains today of Gilbert White's fruit wall.

the exact words – with those White wrote in the *Garden Kalendar*.'

Continuing through the outer garden, we come upon White's sundial, erected by him in 1761, and situated above his ha-ha, 'a fine fence against the Mead'. 'You may remember the piece in the *Garden Kalendar*,' says Mr. Standing in reference to the depth of this sunken fence. 'Gilbert White's labourers

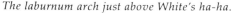
The laburnum arch just above White's ha-ha.

The Herb Garden also includes many plants mentioned by White – scorzonera, flame-leafed parsley, thyme, horseradish, Hamburg parsley (the parsnip-rooted parsley, with a root like a parsnip and the taste of parsley), and skirret, also an umbelliferous Old World plant. Gilbert White had trouble with this unusual, sweet-tasting root crop – it all ran to seed. Here also are soapwort, lemon balm, sage, marjoram, and a number of different mints.

The Rose Garden at The Wakes.

French and African marigolds.

mistook the level, especially about the angle (the protrusion or bastion) and it turned out to be over 6 feet deep at that point, and about 3 or 4 feet deep at either end.' The impending danger of the ha-ha led to chains being put around the bastion piece and a flower border running along it, which rather destroyed the point of the ha-ha as an invisible fence.

Up on the lawn, a short part of its east-west boundary contains what remains of Gilbert White's fruit wall in which is set his inscribed stone, 'G W 1761'. Here he grew five vines, three nectarines, two peach trees and an apricot, and a passion flower adorning each end. Today there are some apricot trees, given by Mr. Nettle, the head gardener at Rotherfield Park with which Gilbert White had connections. Here too are 'Marvel of Peru' (*Mirabilis jalapa*) under which his 7-pound American tortoise,

Timothy, would retreat from the sun. Despite an otherwise assured acceptance that the creation implied a Creator, Gilbert White – forever the empiricist – marvelled that the Almighty had bestowed 'such a profusion of days' on Timothy, 'such a seeming waste of longevity, on a reptile that appears to squander more than two-thirds of its existence in joyless stupor, and be lost to sensation for months together.'

THE GARDEN AT
Shirley

The Reverend William Wilks

'The growth and study of plants is my recreation.'

There were very many fine gardeners among the clergy of the nineteenth century, so many indeed that Dean Hole was once inspired to remark that 'the clergy, as a class, may claim precedence in horticulture . . . in proportion to their numbers, there are more clergymen than laymen who know the difference between a mallow and a salpiglossis, a *Prunus* "Pissardi" and a copper beech.' But at the head of any list of great clergyman horticulturalists must surely be the Reverend William Wilks, who was vicar of Shirley near Croydon in Surrey, from 1880 until 1912.

Wilks was born on October 19th, 1843, and grew up in a family of keen gardeners at Ashford in Kent. Early on he was introduced by a friend to *The Royal Horticultural Society*, and in 1867 he became a Fellow. By 1888 the RHS had got itself into deep financial trouble, the balance sheet showing a debt of £1,152, and they called upon Wilks to become its Secretary. He accepted and persuaded a local man – Mr. Frank Reader, a master at Shirley Boy's School – to abandon teaching and join the RHS as its cashier. Mr. Reader remained cashier for thirty-five years, and together Wilks and Reader reversed the financial fortunes of the society. By 1900 it showed an investment sum of £10,239 and trust funds worth £2,000; and under Wilks's guidance, membership rose from just over 1,000 to 16,000, representing an income of £20,000 a year. He was also the driving force behind the first Chelsea Flower Show and the society's famous garden at Wisley (whose gates today still bear his initials). When Wilks died in 1923, the society's obituary included the words, 'when in one man wisdom is added to knowledge, tact to firm handling of affairs, patience to tenacity of purpose, single-mindedness of aim to ability, knowledge of a man to love of nature and simple things . . . such a man was the Reverend William Wilks.'

Besides his horticultural work, William Wilks was an extremely active priest in the educational, spiritual and material welfare of his parishioners, and gives the lie to the suggestion that the great Victorian clergyman gardeners had little time for their clerical duties. Local historian Miss Nina Foster, who has been going to the church of St. John's in Shirley for as long as she can remember, is one of the few alive today who met him. 'He was a remarkable man, a marvellous parish priest and greatly loved by his people. Shirley in those days was populated mainly by agricultural people. Perhaps he felt he had something in common with them, certainly he had a great understanding of their needs. I remember there was one lady who lived to be 100 but died a couple of years ago, who told me that she recalled Wilks coming to her when she was a little girl, after her grandmother died, carrying an armful of daffodils to put on the coffin – that was the sort of care he showed.

'He recognised the significance of the fact that we had never had a manorial system in Shirley: Shirley people were very independent and didn't like charity. I suppose he would have been considered a bit of a socialist today. He wanted to help his people, so he got the money the parish needed from his wealthy friends but started Clubs so that the poorer of the parish could contribute

Out walking along the southern boundary of his garden one day, William Wilks
chanced upon a mutation of the common field poppy. After ten years
of patient crossing and re-crossing , he developed a new and
now famous strain which he called the Shirley poppy.

to funds and thereby maintain their independence. If you belonged, say, to a Boot Club (for a payment of 1d a week) it meant you were entitled to a pair of boots each year, and so forth. He was especially interested in the employment of his younger parishioners and often included a notice like this in the Parish Magazine: 'August 1889. The Vicar would be very greatly obliged to anyone who could tell of a good place for a young woman of 18 years of age as a kitchenmaid. Also, of an opening for a lad of 16 whom he can himself personally recommend highly – office work or in a gentleman's household or for garden or stable or both.

'Though a bachelor, he loved children, and was way ahead of the times in ecclesiastical procedural matters: he would baptise babies in a pudding basin on the chancel steps so that people could see what was happening and feel part of it, and he drew up a special service book for children so that they could understand what was going on.'

The gates at the RHS garden at Wisley, which bear Wilks's initials and the Shirley poppy.

Shirley was the first garden William Wilks had had to himself. Its initial planning had been done by his predecessor, the Revd. Matthew Farrer, and from a map of 1837 we can calculate that the garden originally covered about 10 acres. Farrer certainly planted the great cedar tree near what is today the garden's south boundary, and almost certainly the holly hedge which still bounds the property along the Upper Shirley Road.

Behind the garden on its southern boundary lay agricultural ground. One day William was walking along this part, gazing at a patch of wild poppies in the field nearby, when he noticed that one flower was different. Wild poppies have been with us since prehistoric times, and *Papaver rhoeas*, the common cornfield poppy – rich red silky petals, black stamen and hairy stem – is regarded as an agricultural weed, albeit a marvellous sight. The petals of the particular poppy that caught the clergyman's notice, however, had *white* edges.

William Wilks climbed into the field, detached the seed capsule of that one poppy flower with its white-edged petals, and sowed the seeds from it in his own garden. From the resulting plants he discarded all 'normal' flowers, and continued the process – getting up early every morning to beat the bees at their own game – until he had cross-bred a whole range of colours from the produce of that original seed pod. It took him ten years' work to produce a range of cultivated poppies varying from brightest scarlet to pure white with all shades of pink in between, and all varieties of flakes and edged flowers with a white base instead of the black base of the wild poppy. The only variety he didn't quite succeed in creating was the blue: apparently some-body just beat him to it. In 1923 he received the first class certificate of the RHS for his achievement.

For a description of the garden we can turn to a contemporary report in *Country Life Illustrated*, May 21st, 1898: 'The vicarage garden of Shirley is in truth a charming parsonage retreat, surrounded for the most part by hedges of holly – healthy, leafy, and we think unrivalled in their way, reaching from 10 to 14 feet in height and 8 feet through, splendid evergreen screens. Our illustrations reveal its character, that of a pretty parsonage home, irregular and artistic, a sweep of velvety turf upon which medlar, quince, apple, cedars, and scarlet oak cast their shadows. There is no formal gardening here, no flower-beds blazing with exotic colouring, no straining after effects, no expensive and elaborate designs – simply the finer perennials and trees, a few from distant lands, but only enough to enhance the beauty of our old home favourites, planted in such a way as to reveal their characteristic beauty. It is a paintable garden.' The writer goes on to describe a woodland walk around the outskirts of the garden, but hidden from view. Clearly from the description the garden extended further south in those days, though there is no record of land sale in this part.

'On the East side of the house, surrounded with the glorious holly hedges of which we have written, is the so-called kitchen garden, but undergoing a rapid change from its former self. Mr. Wilks en-croaches yearly upon the utilitarian plots ... the onward march of daffodils, paeonies, phloxes, irises, and Shirley poppies occupying the ground, until flowers will everywhere spread themselves over this parsonage garden ... One may gather many useful hints in this garden. Phloxes, of which Mr. Wilks has a splendid collection, are grown between the aspar-agus beds. The object of this is to give shade and moisture to the phlox roots which rejoice in a cool damp soil, the feathery asparagus foliage sheltering the roots from hot suns. Over 100 varieties of Chinese paeony find a home here ... there is much beauty in this rich colouring of the young growth, intensified when associated with daffodil and yellow primrose. Hyacinths and tulips were in full flower, and this strong break originated from a stock Mr. Wilks possessed fifteen years ago. We have seldom seen finer spikes in the open ground, and the foliage was broad and strong ...'

In fact, it was at the north-west corner of the garden that Wilks grew his most beautiful spring flowers – wild blue anemones amongst other de-lights. For not only was he interested in garden plants but wild flowers too, and the cornfield poppy was not the only one he cultivated.

Some of the 700 rose bushes in the garden at Shirley.

He also introduced 700 rose trees into the vicarage garden, and between 4 and 6 o'clock on Sunday afternoons his parishioners would walk round the garden to enjoy them. There is indeed a long history of the garden being made use of by the people of the parish. In 1856 we have Wilks's predecessor, Matthew Farrer's description of how they came over to the vicarage after the foundation stone of the new church had been laid, and the children played till half past seven. And we know from the present incumbent, the Revd. Arthur Quinn, that in its somewhat truncated form the garden still welcomes its

William Wilks (centre, eating) and friends enjoying a picnic in the southern part of the garden at Shirley Vicarage, near where he collected the poppy seeds.

parishioners – 'we treat it as a parish asset'.

But the most remarkable occasion was that of Queen Victoria's Jubilee in 1887 when William Wilks proposed that on that day 'all should meet together, high and low, rich and poor, old and young, masters, mistresses and servants, men, women and children

Looking out from Wilks's woodland walk.

The garden of The Wilderness.

'*There is no formal gardening here ... simply the finer perennials and trees, a few from distant lands.*'

for a short Service of rejoicing at 12 o'clock and afterwards, adjourn, if fine, to the vicarage garden for a Village Feast, to which everybody living in the boundary of Shirley Parish is invited.' The weather was indeed fine, and, Nina Foster reports, '735 people sat down for the feast'

Tea followed the feast at 5.30 'the afternoon having been spent at the Fair in the vicarage meadow with side-shows, jugglers, acrobats, etc. and music by the two village bands. After tea, dancing till 9.30 when the *Croydon Advertiser* reported that "the villagers dispersed to their homes all of them well pleased at having spent a most enjoyable and very memorable day." '

When William Wilks retired as vicar of Shirley in 1912, the RHS bought 7 acres of land adjoining the vicarage and built a house for him in appreciation of his work. He called it The Wilderness. Clergymen reading this might consider the prospect of an incumbent, with all his close ties in the community, retiring not only within the parish but *next door* to

the vicarage, a recipe for disaster, especially since Wilks's successor, the Revd. George Jones, was rumoured to be 'different' (a reference to his liturgical practices). But, laughs Miss Foster, 'by all accounts it worked out well. Wilks used to take the 8 a.m. service quite often and always preached at Harvest Festival after he retired. Harvest Festival was always a great thing; I believe the collection used to go to the gardener's benevolent fund!'

Around 1970, some land on the western boundary was sold by Canterbury Diocese and a bungalow built where the wild spring garden had been. Not long after, more land was sold, this time most of the original kitchen garden on the eastern boundary. In 1983, as Arthur Quinn describes, a further alteration was carried out: 'It was decided that the old house was too big and costly. The Authorities thought that they could sell the house with a large plot of land and get an enormous sum for it. But we've got a very active Conservation group in Croydon and as soon as they heard that the house was on the market they managed to get it listed, and practically all the trees have preservation orders on them now. At the time of writing the house is still unsold.'

Today the Revd. Quinn, who has been vicar of Shirley since 1974, can look across a fence which divides his compact living quarters from the home where his children grew up – fairly ripping the old garden in two. The effect is extraordinary to behold, for both the lay of the land and its plants still decree that the garden should remain one; its fence is not 'open' and planted with young climbing plants in an effort to merge the two in a natural way, but bald, woven wood severely secured by concrete pillars. A saddening sight.

THE GARDEN AT
Ludgvan

The Reverend Canon Arthur Townshend Boscawen

'It will be a happy thing for Cornwall if his example inspires many others, both clergy and laity, to seek the same paths of sympathetic co-operation with Nature and with their fellow-men.'

Bishop Joseph Wellington Hunkin

Arthur Townshend Boscawen became Rector of Ludgvan, just east of Penzance, in 1893. The village (its name pronounced locally without the 'v' and with a soft 'g') first earned its place in botanical records when William Borlase, rector there between 1722 and 1772, wrote his classic work, *The Natural History of Cornwall.*

One of Boscawen's crimson manukas for which he won a Gold Medal from the Royal Horticultural Society.
Canon Boscawen with Eucryphia Nymansay.

Revue Horticole

Nouvelles variétés de Leptospermum Scoparium
A. Nicholsii·B. Boscawenii

Ludgvan Rectory, 1942 and 1987. 'The lawn slopes down between belts of trees and outlying palms striding onto the grass, and here and there a tall shrub marooned.' F. Kingdon Ward

Boscawen learned his horticultural skills at Lamorran from his famous gardening father, the Hon. Revd. J.T. Boscawen. In 1895 he became a fellow of *The Royal Horticultural Society*. From 1898 he judged pretty constantly at RHS shows, as well as being the moving spirit behind many local shows. In 1912 he won the Gold Medal and *The Gardener's Chronicle* Cup for New Plants, and subsequently introduced two daffodils into horticulture: 'St Ludgvan' and one named after his daughter, 'Karena', a Cornish word meaning 'love'. His crowning glory came in 1922 when he was awarded the society's ultimate accolade, the Victoria Medal of Honour.

The 1912 Cup was awarded for six crimson manukas, *Leptospermum scoparium* 'Nichollsii', raised in the rectory garden from seed sent from New Zealand. It is an unusual variety to which is

'It is a remarkable feature of this garden that the very rocks are covered with clinging carpets of woody plants.' F. Kingdon Ward, 1929

'If you get shelter you can grow almost anything on the shores of Mounts Bay.' Canon Boscawen

attached an intriguing story of discovery. Apparently only a single plant of it was found wild in its home country. 'It was a large shrub,' reported Mr. J. Drummond in the *Auckland Weekly News* in 1923, 'and it grew conspicuously in a white manuka copse on a sandy prominence at Chaney's, about a mile from the River Styx, and about 6 miles from Christchurch.' The copse belonged to a Mr. W.P. Spencer, and on the day he first noticed it he took a sprig for his buttonhole on his way to a meeting with a Mr. W. Nicholls in Christchurch. Spencer was eager to do business with Nicholls, and when the latter admired his buttonhole, Spencer made him a present of it. Later that day Nicholls happened to be visiting a nursery and the sprig again attracted attention, this time from the nursery owner, one Mr. R. Nairn. Measuring the situation carefully, Nicholls refused to say where it had come from, but subsequently provided Nairn with cuttings from Spencer's bush. Thus the variety came into cultivation and was known henceforth as 'Nichollsii'! Not Spencer's lucky day, and one can only hope that his other business with Nicholls proved more profitable.

The Gardener's Chronicle cup was accompanied by a prize of 25 guineas, which like other considerable sums provided by his special interest, Boscawen consigned to the restoration of Ludgvan Church. But from the start, the Canon's vision was inspired by more than accolades or prize money. Time and again he connected his horticultural wisdom with the enhancement of life in Cornwall. Early in his ministry, he had the idea of establishing different kinds of heather to cheer up the embankments of the encroaching railroad, and to this day specimens of *Erica lusitanica* can be seen near the line at Dobwalls in East Cornwall. Later, in glebe land just south of the rectory garden, he took to growing anemones, succeeding with them on a commercial scale and thereby founding the still thriving Cornish anemone industry.

Looking towards St. Michael's Mount, across the field where Boscawen grew his anemones.

But perhaps his greatest single achievement in this way was his enterprise in broccoli. Boscawen noticed that the English broccoli business was not at all successful, the plants were poor. So, he imported seed from Bavaria and distributed it to certain Cornish farmers on the condition that they grow it purely for seed for a period of three or four years. At the appointed time the English market was flooded with the home-grown Cornish broccoli, and a second great Cornish industry was born.

Fitting in these activities with his work as a parish priest couldn't have been easy especially as Boscawen worked his own 2-acre garden with only one assistant, often downing tools and racing across to the church for wedding or funeral before returning with not a moment wasted.

Far from interfering with his work, however, his passion for plants was seen by his bishop as an inextricable aspect of his vocation. The Bishop recalled: 'His life was a shining example of the combination of personal faith and practical usefulness, of work and play, of beauty and fruitfulness, of activity and peace . . . it will be a happy thing for Cornwall if his example inspires many others, both clergy and laity, to seek the same paths of sympathetic co-operation with Nature and with their fellow-men.'

Boscawen's parishioners responded by packing the church even on the least popular occasions. Visiting preachers to his regular week-day service throughout Lent (hardly the most rousing period in the Church Calendar) were surprised and delighted to find a full and attentive congregation assembled in their working clothes. Even the children of the parish, to each of whom he had given a silver christening mug, fell under his spell. The Hon. Mrs. H. E. Boscawen, told us of a chance meeting with an elderly lady who attended Sunday School in the Canon's time. 'The lady recalled how as children they would be taken, after Sunday School, into the rectory garden to see the flowers. On one special occasion they were challenged to memorise the difficult name of a particularly splendid flower. "I remember it to this day," she said, and spelt it out for me, "P-U-Y-A C-H-I-L-E-N-S-I-S!"' This almost certainly occurred in the year 1916, for we learn from another source that this was the year in which Boscawen's spectacular plant sent up a flower spike nearly 12ft. high at Ludgvan rectory. Incidentally, Mrs. Boscawen's own mighty acreage at The High Beeches, Handcross in Surrey (a landscape originally laid out by Sir Robert Loder in 1849) is an awesome example of what the Boscawens do by way of gardening today and is open to the public on certain days.

Here in the 'ultima Thule of the West Country,' recalled the famous plant explorer, F. Kingdon Ward in March, 1929, Boscawen created, 'a small garden of exquisite beauty, where trees and shrubs from the southern hemisphere grow with a will; a garden which fulfils the ideal of a garden which is not a mere museum, so that we may walk round it three times, and see it with new eyes each time.'

Like his father before him, Arthur Boscawen's chief interest lay in trees and shrubs and he was heavily influenced by the flora of the Antipodes, relying for supply upon a brother he had in the New Zealand Forestry Commission and a strong relationship with Mr. T.F. Cheeseman, who was Curator of the Auckland Museum and an important source of both information and seeds.

In his Antipodean collection were many pittosporums, the New Zealand beech (*Nothofagus fusca*), *Myrtus bullata* and *M. obcordata*, a number of the flowering shrub *Hoheria spp.*, and he had the first *Olearia semidentata* ever to flower in this country, one of seventeen different varieties of the plant which, at Ludgvan Rectory, formed the finest collection in England. There were also senecios ('Among the best I have of the New Zealand species is *Senecio* "Hectori",' he wrote in 1923) and metrosideros ('The best of these are *M. lucida* and *M. robusta* . . . They are not affected by wind or the salt spray near the coast; they

Senecio 'Monroi'.

Olearia semidentata.

are beautiful in habit and growth.'), all more suited to the mild climate of the south-west than anywhere else in England.

Ludgvan faces south and west on a shelf of rising ground a mile from the Atlantic and in view of St. Michael's Mount. In his description of the garden, Kingdon Ward notes that although not entirely frost free, 'its chief enemy is the south-west wind, which so many of our soft, west coast districts suffer.' But Boscawen's art had been absorbed as a child at Lamorran, and the importance of good shelter had not been lost on him: 'The first, second and third thing to remember is to get shelter. If you can get shelter you can grow almost anything on the shores of Mounts Bay,' Boscawen once declared.

'The lawn,' continued Kingdon Ward, 'slopes

Pittosporum eugenioides.

Mrs. Parsons adds scale to some of Boscawen's palm trees.

down [from the house] between belts of trees with outlying palms striding on to the grass, and here and there a tall shrub marooned. Winding paths thread the massed vegetation, and suddenly the visitor comes on a bulge of rock work overflowing with wide waves of precious creeper, or descends into a grotto whose angular slopes are planted with metallic foliage. For it is a remarkable feature of this garden, devoted to trees and shrubs, that the very rocks are covered with clinging carpets of woody plants . . .'

Today, on the garden's rocky outcrops a modern rectory has been built. The present incumbent, the Reverend Arthur Parsons, and his wife are both keen gardeners and determined to re-create in what is but one half (the southern part) of the original rectory grounds some of the beauty of those days at Ludgvan. But he is not permitted to 'spoil' the view

of St. Michael's Mount by putting up a windbreak, and sadly the serious winter of 1986 wrought havoc on both his and some of Boscawen's own plantings, including, almost certainly, one of Boscawen's favourite plants a *Pittosporum eugenioides* that had earlier, miraculously, managed to survive the building of the new house.

Arthur Boscawen died in 1939. At the end, when he was paralysed and almost speechless after a stroke, a friend spoke to him about the great frost that had so injured his favourite lily-of-the-valley tree, *Clethra arborea*. With great effort, and faith in its recuperative powers, he managed to make himself understood with the words, 'It'll come.' Sure enough, after he died, the huge tree, probably the largest ever to grow in this country, began to break vigorously near its base.

Fairseat

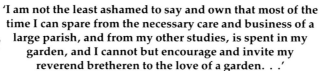

The Reverend and Mrs. David Clark

'I am not the least ashamed to say and own that most of the time I can spare from the necessary care and business of a large parish, and from my other studies, is spent in my garden, and I cannot but encourage and invite my reverend bretheren to the love of a garden. . .'

The Revd. John Laurence in The Clergyman's Recreation (1714)

It would be a mistake to assume that the Reverend David Clark is a collector of rare plants for the sake of it, that his interest is purely scientific, though his plant lists and planting plans are bound to make his contribution appear the most technical. The care with which he and his wife have thought out and arranged colour combinations and contrasts of texture and form is the real mark of the garden's success, but it is an artistic creation which has evolved with the growth of his scientific knowledge, one continually inspiring the other. The results have to be seen to be believed and fortunately can be, as the garden is open to the public on certain dates in June and July.

The Clarks moved to Fairseat, situated a few miles from Sevenoaks in Kent, in 1969; it was a very small parish (only 550 people altogether). The rectory was described as temporary accomodation because up until then the rector had lived in the sister parish of Standstead and the house there had

just been sold. But the plan to build a small replacement never materialised, and instead, in 1977, Fairseat Rectory became the focal point of a greatly expanded parish to include Vigo village, a modern estate with an additional population of 2,000.

In the intervening years, 1969 to 1977, David Clark had become a serious gardener. The background was there, his father, a veterinary surgeon use to open their garden to the public when David was a boy: 'He didn't marry until he was forty-two, by which time he had bought several building plots at Felixstowe in East Suffolk. There he built his home, a tennis court and a garden, and then got married. Later, both my sister and I were given a small bed each, and pretty soon I became keen on growing vegetables. You see quick results with vegetables – start to finish in six weeks – and it meant extra pocket money for me. I would sow the sweetcorn at the end of the Easter holidays and the cloches would be ready for harvesting at the beginning of August, when I would sell the produce in local shops.'

Soon after they arrived in Fairseat, David and his wife, Alison, joined the local horticultural society and have shown at exhibition virtually ever since, recently concentrating on pinks and dahlias. David also gives talks to luncheon clubs, horticultural and flower arranging societies.

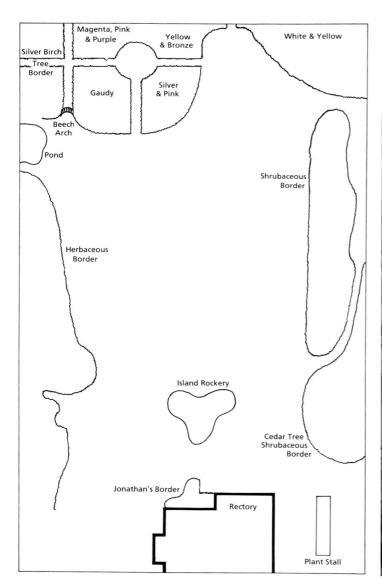

Left, plan of the garden beds and borders.

Below, Lupinus 'Chandelier' from the herbaceous border.

The shrubaceous border – (front) Dianthus 'Mrs. Sinkins' and purple petunia, (middle) violet blue geranium and the creamy shrub Euonymus fortunei 'Silver Queen', with Digitalis purpurea and Cotinus coggygria 'Notcutt's Variety' in the background.

The garden itself is relatively small, about two-thirds of an acre. In 1969 it consisted of five or six rose beds and a very narrow herbaceous border 'with miles of grass edges to cut'. Today he has twelve island and hedge-backed beds, each dedicated to a theme or idea which has been carefully and imaginatively planted.

The first development was one of two 'shrubaceous' borders, an island bed of shrubs and perennials. On the day in late June when the photographs were taken we were struck by the tall blue poppy, *Meconopsis baileyi* 'Branklyn', the blue penstemons and *Primula vialii*; the contrast of yellow jasmine with a big reddish cotinus, the clear crimson reds of a sprawling potentilla that had been carefully tied to 'bunch' the effect so successfully.

Nearby, a huge cedar provided dappled shade for a cool planting of hostas, ferns, juniper, dead nettle and foxglove . . . But what now began to unfold, as we walked down the garden, made us wish that we could leave a photographer at Fairseat for months on end to catch the successive high points as they occurred. Here in various stages of development were a 'white and yellow' border (the result of a visit to Sissinghurst), a 'yellow and bronze' border (inspired by the garden at Crathes Castle near Aberdeen), a 'silver and pink' border, another shamelessly described by its gardener as 'gaudy – hot colours', a 'magenta, pink and purple' border, an island rockery, and a bed reserved for son Jonathan's plantings – he is a student at Hadlow Horticultural College.

David's ideas for themes or combinations come from other gardens and articles he reads. From his study on the first floor of the rectory he looks down on his creation and constantly ruminates over the success or future possibilities of new combinations of colour and form. He belongs to *The Hardy Plant Society* and finds their book, *The Plant Finder* (which tells you where to buy any plant you want), absolutely indispensable. Eager to share his experience, he prepares meticulous border plans, each plant keyed in, so that when the crowds arrive on open days they can make notes of what they like before delving into *The Plant Finder* to discover where it can be bought.

The garden is open under the National Gardens Scheme. But the public days began, simply, with lilies. In 1970 David decided to grow a number from seed 'and two years later the martegons started flowering. Suddenly we realised that we had quite a display of lilies in July, and 1973 was in fact the first year that we had the garden open.' He describes the legions of visitors as 'indomitable. We were open last Sunday week and it had been raining on and off all day and was still pouring at 12.45, yet by 4p.m., 260 people were in the garden drinking tea, studying the plants, and occasionally standing motionless with their umbrellas up until a downpour stopped.'

Right, looking through the beech arch to the herbaceous border. Below, the herbaceous border. Below right, Aquilegia 'McKana' hybrids.

Opposite, left, a section of the white and yellow bed, including Rosa 'Blanc Double de Coubert' in the foreground, Potentilla davurica veitchii and Geranium sanguineum album behind, with a spike of Morina longifolia just visible in the background. Opposite, right, Morina longifolia.

Plant lists

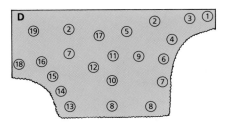

1 *Alyssum saxatile* 'Dudley Neville'
2 Golden yew
3 *Tovara* 'Painter's Palette'
4 Violas 'Chantryland' and 'Irish Molly'
5 *Melissa* 'Aurea'
6 *Geum* 'Copper Tone'
7 *Heuchera micrantha* 'Palace Purple'
8 *Limnanthes douglasii*
9 *Euphorbia amygdaloides rubra*
10 *Phygelius aequalis*
11 *Berberis thunbergii* 'Aurea'
12 *Salvia officinalis* 'Purpurascens'
13 Hakonechloa
14 *Sedum rhodiola*
15 *Aster rotundifolius*
16 Bowles' golden grass
17 *Helichrysum petiolatum* 'Aureum'
18 *Mertensia pterocarpa*
19 *Polemonium caeruleum*

E – Silver and Pink
1 *Helianthemum* 'Wisley Pink'
2 *Salvia officinalis* 'Tricolor'
3 *Hypericum x moserianum* 'Tricolor'
4 *Abelia floribunda*
5 *Rosa* 'Frau Dagmar Hartopp'
6 *Salvia argentea*
7 *Geranium traversii elegans*
8 *Astrantia carniolica rubra*
9 *Chrysanthemum haradjani*
10 *Artemisia splendens*
11 *Cistus x purpureus*
12 *Salvia grahamii*
13 *Weigela florida* 'Foliis Purpureis'
14 *Stachys olympica*
15 *Artemisia lanata*
16 *Cistus x skanbergii*
17 *Pyrethrum ptarmicifolium*
18 *Senecio leucostachys*

Above, Lilium martagon album in the white border. Above right, the gaudy border – (front) Geum 'Mrs. Bradshaw',

Potentilla 'Yellow Queen', (middle) Mimulus cardinalis, (back) Erysimum 'Wenlock Beauty'.

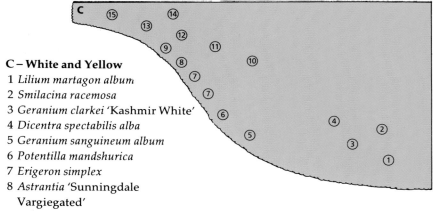

C – White and Yellow

1 *Lilium martagon album*
2 *Smilacina racemosa*
3 *Geranium clarkei* 'Kashmir White'
4 *Dicentra spectabilis alba*
5 *Geranium sanguineum album*
6 *Potentilla mandshurica*
7 *Erigeron simplex*
8 *Astrantia* 'Sunningdale Vargiegated'
9 *Pulmonaria* 'Sissinghurst White'
10 *Robinia* 'Frisia'
11 *Philadelphus coronarius variegatus*
12 *Aquilegia* 'Nora Barlow'
13 *Potentilla davurica veitchii*

14 *Choisya ternata*
15 *Rosa* 'Blanc Double de Coubert' with *Lamium* 'White Nancy' underneath.

Above, Dutch irises midst matricaria and Berberis thunbergii 'Aurea' in the yellow and bronze bed. Left, Primula vialii, one of the most beautiful of all primulas, grows in perfect company with blue Penstemon ovatus and orangey Primula 'Inshriach' hybrid.

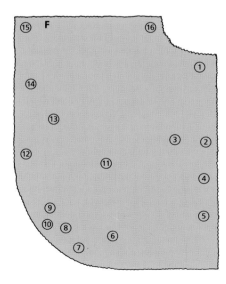

F – Gaudy

1 *Euryops acraeus*
2 *Geum* 'Borisii'
3 *Potentilla* 'Daydawn'
4 *P.* 'Yellow Queen'
5 *P.* 'Mrs. Bradshaw'
6 *Cheiranthus* 'E.K. Emshirst'
7 A mimulus medley
8 *Fuchsia* 'Genii'
9 *Potentilla* 'Red Ace'
10 *Origanum vulgare aureum*
11 *Rosa moyesii* 'Geranium'
12 *Helianthemum* 'Henfield Brilliant'
13 *Symphoricarpos orbiculatus*
14 *Erysimum* 'Wenlock Beauty'
15 Nemesia
16 Marigold 'Nell Gwyn'

THE GARDEN AT
Lustleigh

The Reverend and Mrs. Edwin Deacon

'Once taste the delights of a garden, and they will never fail to please. The cloud, no bigger than a man's hand, shall be followed by a gracious and abundant rain.'

Samuel Reynolds Hole

Lustleigh is everything a Devon village ought to be but rarely is; perhaps its total absence from some road maps (ours, at least) has gone some way to preserve it. Its acidic Dartmoor soil, product of volcanic eruptions in days gone by, favours the growth of rhododendrons, azaleas, heaths and heathers, but is less kind to roses, so we visited in May, and caught the rectory garden at its best.

Laid out for easy maintenance during a period of

sixteen years by the Reverend and Mrs. Edwin Deacon, Lustleigh is a steeply sloping garden of trees and shrubs, lawns and terraced walkways which meander through spreading ground coverers and brightly coloured feature plants. Today, fully justifying its conception, the garden is kept in trim, just one day a week, by a gardener employed by the present non-gardening residents, the Reverend and Mrs. Kenneth Jackson.

Now in retirement in nearby Highweek Village, Edwin Deacon recalls that when he and his family arrived in June 1969, 'it was in a pretty parlous state, the whole area covered with trees and shrubs and no lawn at all. We visited it on two or three occasions before we even discovered the summer house, which was worm eaten and which I burnt on sight. Canon Newman and his wife used to breakfast in it, but he became a very sick man and let the whole garden go, and his successor, the Reverend McGee, was too elderly to get to grips with it.

'We had a tractor in and grubbed up these enormous tree roots, and cleared the face of the house because you couldn't see out of the windows for the creepers over them. Incredible, for the views from the house are marvellous. We planted the lawn and never had to treat it in the sixteen years we were there, just mowed it every week or ten days in season. On the first two or three cuttings I'd take the grass off and compost it, then from May to September, when it was warm, I'd leave the grass on as mulch, composting the last few cuttings of the year.

'The rhodos on the east side were a bit of a mistake. I planted them beside a dry stone boundary wall that looks onto the lane, but they like plenty of moisture and might have done better further down towards the drive; still, they've been there for about ten or twelve years. People used to stop and ask if

A terraced walkway through a bank of heathers for all seasons.

once more.' Fortunately, Edwin discovered someone for whom the labour brought its own refreshment.

'Eventually it all got too much and my wife, Rosemary, proved herself to be a very good digger. In fact she ended up doing most of the digging; she likes it, I don't know why.' Rosemary's own remembrance is that her digging the kitchen garden began 'out of necessity, there being no one else available.' But over the years she found it very rewarding: 'It gave me a real sense of achievement when the garden produced bumper crops. When crops failed owing to weather, disease or uninvited "visitors", it helped me to be patient, better able to accept disappointments.'

In fact, the garden was very much a shared occupation – Edwin would do all the trimming of the hedges, mow the lawn and do the pruning, staking and sowing of seeds, and Rosemary would do the digging and planting of shrubs and trees 'because she's got green fingers. But we'd choose the plants together. We didn't have a master plan, we'd buy just as our fancy took us. I'd make sure we'd have plenty of colour in winter when there aren't any flowers about, colour from all sorts of different firs – pinks, blues and greens, and we found a good and very knowledgeable nurseryman, a Pole who came over in the war and stayed. He and his wife would replace

Rosa 'Golden Showers' climbing the rectory's south face.

they could take pictures of the apricot azalea; my wife reckons it must have been the fiery bush that Moses saw because when you get the westerly sun setting on it, the bush is absolutely like a flame of fire.

'It was a hard garden to work because of the steep incline. Beyond the rhododendrons, on the east side of the top garden, we had a hedge of privet, oak, holly, and laurustinus, which couldn't be cut with hedge trimmers, so we had to use shears and perch on top of a ladder, moving it bit by bit all the way up the steep hill outside. And when we came to digging out the kitchen garden on the western side (it hadn't been tilled for years and was home for countless sycamores, beastly things), we had a terrible time. I had one of those little diggers and started by working downwards, but that simply drove the earth down the hill, so I could only work upwards, getting the machine out of its rut at the top and coasting down again, backwards, endeavouring to stop before plunging over the retaining wall, and then digging in

Acer palmatum 'Aureum'.

anything that failed, and of course hardly anything ever did because they were so good.

'We had all the usual vegetables, choosing Home Guard for our early crop potatoes because that's what the local farmers grow. Always watch what the local farmers plant because they've been there for generations. The Brussels didn't do too well because the soil is so light and they like a heavy soil, and we had to give up growing carrots because the badgers would just come in and woof them. We couldn't stop them. One desperate year there was a terrible drought and the badgers even went for the parsnips, *very* unusual. We were never able to find out where they came in, which is odd because they leave tracks. I even had a man in from Lustleigh who was a tracker and knew all about them.

'Again, we couldn't grow strawberries because the squirrels would come. They'd pounce just as the fruit was about to turn red – they didn't really want them, but they'd go through the netting and pick them off,

The acidic soil is a perfect medium for Edwin Deacon's rhododendron planting on the east side of the rectory although these plants generally do best with less free drainage. The close-up is the 'Moses bush', orange-red Rhododendron calendulaceum, backed by Prunus dulcis.

The Weigela florida 'Variegata' is the focus of attention in a mass of colourful junipers and heathers. Right, beyond the broom on the west lawn, is the Bramley apple.

stacking them in neat little heaps like cannon balls used to be stacked. There was a great deal of wildlife at Lustleigh, umpteen varieties of birds; we even had woodpeckers on the front lawn.

'We grew loganberries on the top wall, and raspberries of course, and apples including a lovely red Bramley on the west lawn; there were two but one was lost in that drought. It blossomed the following year and the leaves came, but then it perished. You often don't know what damage a drought has done until the following year. The Bramley is a cooker, of course, but after Christmas you can eat it as a dessert apple. It's juicy, and it's gorgeous to sit by a log fire in winter and have one of those. Do tell the Jacksons when you see them.'

THE GARDEN AT
St. Feock

The Reverend Ernest Saunders

**'Such successful results can only be expected where the
gardener not merely understands but loves his business.'**

The Reverend Canon Thomas Phillpotts

Our guide through most of the gardens in Cornwall has been the Reverend Ernest Saunders, a considerable gardener and horticulturalist and, from 1963 until his retirement, vicar of St. Feock, a mainly residential parish situated at the mouth of the river Fal across the water from Lamorran. Today he is retired and lives with his wife in a cottage on a steep hillside, part of the Looe Valley near Liskeard.

His garden is planned to appease some special topographical and climatic problems. 'I call it my "Trinitarian garden" because it has been possible to provide path access on three levels,' he'll tell you, swiftly adding that of course in *that* sphere is found no difference of position, 'whilst here it is from lowest to highest! Valleys are very sheltered places, generally, but notorious for heavy frost and I find it is intensely so here. I can no longer grow the tender things I grew at St. Feock. Varieties of viburnum do exceedingly well (some can be very beautiful and scented too), and the later

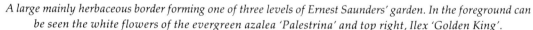

*A large mainly herbaceous border forming one of three levels of Ernest Saunders' garden. In the foreground can
be seen the white flowers of the evergreen azalea 'Palestrina' and top right, Ilex 'Golden King'.*

flowering deciduous azaleas and rhododendrons are generally all right provided the sloping ground doesn't become too dry.' The results are very impressive, and we are not surprised to learn later that this garden has been the subject of a BBC television programme.

Inside the cottage, the atmosphere bubbles with Cornish good humour and joy, and I have to turn the conversation to the specific subject in hand, Cornwall's foremost living clergyman gardener: Born on the family farm, of which this cottage was once part, Ernest learned about plants as a teenager in charge of the family's large vegetable garden. Pretty soon he developed a distinct preference and aptitude for ornamental gardening, and by the age of twenty was exhibiting in the floral sections of Liskeard's horticultural society shows. By thirty-six, when he left the farm and entered the Ministry, his local reputation had been made. Theological training and curacies necessitated a break in exhibiting, but when he was appointed parish priest of St. Keverne with Coverack (two delightfully unspoilt villages on the Lizard Peninsula), he began to specialise in large-flowered gladioli. Medals and cups now litter the shelves at Trussell Cottage, and when pressed, Ernest will tell how he beat the British gladioli champion at the prestigious Camborne Show or amuse you with stories of the 'cards-to-the-chest' competitive spirit among the locals, always suspicious that a visiting 'expert' never really divulges the secrets of his prize-winning form. Following a lecture on the subject of 'Growing Gladioli for Shows', in which Ernest had run through the whole gamut of varieties, soil preparation, fertilisers, planting, feeding, staking, and answered searching questions afterwards, his wife overheard one member say to another, ' 'E idn giving away much tonight, is uh master . . .'

Being close to the famous flower farm at Lanarth, Ernest began to collect narcissi – the Williams family who run it are known nationally for their many hybrids of the bulb. And by 1963 when he moved to St. Feock, his collection of around fifty varieties of excellent show-quality narcissi had taken pride of place. Some of Cornwall's most prestigious cups followed, and Ernest was invited to judge at County shows – 'I admit to being interested in casting a critical eye on other people's efforts,' he says today, but still marvels at what his hobby has become.

'The vicarage at St. Feock stands on a promontory commanding glorious views of the Fal River and Carrick Roads or Falmouth Harbour; windows on the North overlook a well-wooded creek called Pill. The garden, I estimate, covers at least half an acre. It had a few fine trees, including a red ornamental chestnut, red-flowered crataegus (hawthorn), a *Robinia frisia*, a cupressus and fir or two. I retained the big lawn and renewed the flower beds around, planting a beech hedge where there had been concrete posts and wire before. To the right as one looked seaward, a "secret" garden totally derelict sloped down to a small valley. This I turned into what became an area of flowering shrubs, some donated for the purpose, many propagated from cuttings, and others provided by friends with excellent collections in the parish. I must mention one magnolia, named 'Lanarth', and given to me when about 4 feet high by Mr. Michael Williams. Over the years it grew to some 20 feet high, and was said to flower at 12 to 14 years of age. I was at St. Feock nearly fourteen years, and towards the end I came to the conclusion that posterity would

An outstanding specimen of Pieris formosa 'Wakehurst' against the wall of the Revd. Saunders' cottage.

Potentillas – fruticosa in the foreground and 'Red Ace' just visible beneath the lovely broom, Cytisus praecox 'Allgold'. The rhododendron is R. 'Winsome'.

A small, less formal variety of Papaver orientale.

have to benefit from its flowering. But in the last spring I was there, it gave me its first glorious burst of bloom. I believed I deserved that after all my care!'

Conversation strays onto the history of the parish and, in particular, a vicar who can lay claim to being St. Feock's most famous churchman – Canon Thomas Phillpotts. Like Ernest Saunders, Thomas Phillpotts (who was vicar of St. Feock from 1844) showed an early interest in gardening and rose to become a judge at local flower shows. Between 1838 and 1840 he judged at least four times in the Cottage Garden Section of *The Royal Horticultural Society* shows at Truro and Falmouth, and later became Steward for the horticultural section of the famous Bath and West Show.

Thomas Phillpotts took up residence not in the vicarage where Ernest lived, but at a house called Porthgwidden which his father had bought in 1842. Thomas Phillpotts Sr. was a wealthy barrister and M.P. for Gloucester, and owned a prestigious London residence at 14 Pall Mall. Thomas's personality was clearly influenced by the cosmopolitan culture in which he grew up. His was a decisive even pragmatic nature and he could call on resources that were at once both deeper and more farflung than most Cornish country clergymen. Almost his first action as vicar was to build and part finance an additional church at Devoran because he noticed that a large part of his congregation lived nearer there than Feock. The architect he hired came from London and was called John Loughborough Pearson, the man who later, and as a result of Thomas's own singular efforts, built the great Cathedral at Truro. Thomas's uncle was Bishop Phillpotts of Exeter at a time when there was no separate diocese for the Cornish. It is safe to say that Thomas, who became one of the first Canons of the new diocese, spared none of his considerable energy in pushing the Bishop into a decision that Exeter should be divided into two separate sees: Truro (for Cornwall) and Exeter (for Devon).

Porthgwidden looks down upon the estuary from which the River Fal flows into the sea. In the mid-nineteenth century it contained eight good-sized bedrooms as well as the usual dining and drawing rooms, library and 'boudoir', two kitchens, housekeeper's room, servants' bedrooms, and so on. Its name means 'the White Haven', supposedly due to the colour of the sand on the beach at the bottom of the garden.

A contemporary description mentions 'a productive garden, orchard, meadow and arable land . . . with about eight acres of walks and pleasure gardens interspersed with Timber Trees, shrubberies and

Looking towards the Fal estuary, over the 'white sands'. This was the site of the first floral exhibition ever to be staged by the RHS outside London, and despite all Canon Phillpotts' efforts, 'at four o'clock the rain started and there was a general scamper for shelter'.

thriving plantations, and with a large lawn shelving to the river.' Dean Hole chose it for description in *A Book About the Garden*: 'The garden at Porthgwidden, with its pleasant paths, conducting you from the fair home above to the banks and bathing-place below, amid rare trees, and shrubs, and flowers, gracefully arranged and tended with skilful care, is one of the most charming of our culture's grounds, reminding us of Spencer's words –

> *It was a chosen plot of fertile land,*
>   *Amid wild waves set like a little nest,*
> *As if it had by Nature's cunning hand*
>   *Been choicely picked out from all the rest.'*

We know from a present occupant, Dr. George Lee, that in 1851 Thomas Phillpotts enjoyed the services of six female servants, two governesses, one male servant, a laundress, butler, coachman and bailiff at Porthgwidden, and one could be forgiven for wondering how much gardening was left for Thomas to do. But the truth is that he did get involved, and his interest was at once scientific and pastoral.

His passion was his greenhouses, which he erected in 1850 and a full report of which is contained in *The Journal of The Royal Horticultural Society*, Volume vii, part i. In one house he grew in quick succession pot vines, melons, cucumbers, etc., and in

another, he grew orchids: 'a choice collection of these lovely luxuries, which are beyond my exchequer and experience,' Dean Hole admits, 'and of which I only

Porthgwidden – 'about 8 acres of walks and pleasure gardens interspersed with Timber Trees, shrubberies and thriving plantations.'

Odontoglossum 'Alexandrae'.

Cypripedium niveum.

remember *Odontoglossum* "Alexandrae", and amid countless beautiful *Cypripediums, hirsutum,* "Lowi", and *niveum.*'

But it was the method of heating his houses which was Thomas's great invention. He was conscious that the perfect greenhouse system depends upon good ventilation plus the right proportion of light, moisture and heat. In particular he was concerned that increasing the temperature of his houses by artificial means would dry out the atmosphere, and that decreasing it by admitting outside air would create too sudden an effect that would damage his plants. So, he built an air chamber between the two houses connecting it to them by means of a series of drains; air passed over the surface of warming pipes and into the pits via six-inch square, perforated zinc gratings. This eliminated draughts, ensured that the outside air had lost its chill and, with the addition of open water troughs, allowed sufficient moisture into

Polgwynne. The patio is planted with heathers and conifers, its retaining wall bedecked with an ancient wistaria.

Canon Phillpotts' greenhouses, erected in 1850.

The patio at Polgwynne gives onto a self-contained shrub garden, brimming this May day with the cheery colours of deciduous azaleas – Exbury hybrids.

the atmosphere for an optimum growing environment.

Pastorally, Thomas believed fervently in the spiritual benefit of gardening. Like Charles Dickens' friend, the philanthropist Miss Burdett-Coutts who campaigned at this time for the improvement of cottage gardens, window boxes for town houses, and especially allotments, he exercised great efforts in recommending gardening as a natural balance to the materialistic motives engendered by the Industrial Revolution. On August 30th, 1859, he organised and staged an exhibition by *The Royal Horticultural Society* at Porthgwidden, the first ever to be staged outside London. According to a pamphlet published

by the Feock Local History Group, 'Crowds came by road and by the steamers from Truro; the Miners Artillery Band played on the lawn in front of the house; the Exhibits were in a marquee to the south east, by the archery ground. Refreshments were served in another marquee and after lunch there were speeches.' In his opening address Thomas

Dazzling white lilies rise from the inky depths of the pond at Polgwynne.

Polgwynne's lower lawn, and shrub bank of heaths with daboecia, Ceanothus prostratus and Potentilla 'Daydawn'.

stressed the advantages of cottage gardens – 'even drunkards have been reclaimed by work in them;' and declared that the aim of the exhibiton was 'to show the cottager how he could improve his condition and bring comfort to his family.'

In the beginning it was a great success, and apparently the flower judge was so impressed by the Cottage exhibitors that he offered to give them free seeds. But at four o'clock it started to rain and there was a 'general scamper for shelter', the exhibition never to be resumed. Indeed so devastating was the downpour that it washed out any chance of future

Royal Horticultural Society exhibitions in Cornwall.

When Canon Phillpotts retired as vicar of Feock in 1874, after thirty years service, he converted a large part of the grounds into a walled garden which today contains a separate house called Polgwynne, the home of two master gardeners, Mr. and Mrs. P. Davey, whose garden is the subject of many of the accompanying photographs. The Daveys open Polgwynne to the public, their work a most fitting memorial to Porthgwidden's great gardening past.

A statue of Canon Phillpotts outside the south porch of Truro Cathedral. He holds a model of the porch because he personally donated the funds for its construction.

An ancient, sprawling rhododendron, constant companion for the only female ginkgo to be found in England, according to the international tree expert, Alan Mitchell.

THE GARDEN AT
Caunton

Dean Samuel Reynolds Hole

**'Get a man into the fresh air, interest him in the
marvellous works of his God, instead of the deformities of
vice, give him an occupation which will add to his health
and the comforts of his family, instead of destroying both,
then build Revealed upon Natural Religion and hope to
see him a Christian.'**

Caunton Manor where Dean Hole lived as curate and then vicar of Caunton.

In 1844 the Reverend Samuel Reynolds Hole became curate, then, between 1850 and 1887, vicar of Caunton near Newark in Nottinghamshire; subsequently he was appointed Dean of Rochester Cathedral. His was a dramatic personality; everything he did was carried out with great zeal. He was a lover of all vigorous country sports – riding, hunting and archery, and early in his life he had quite a reputation as a *bon viveur*. But he was also blessed with great imagination and sensitivity, and this combination took him to the top in practically everything he set out to do and made him a particularly effective preacher.

In the last century Caunton was home to a small farming community on the banks of a stream called The Beck, some 6 miles of flat farmland north west of Newark. Today the village does not seem a great deal larger than it was then, its Mediaeval church, two public houses (one named the Dean Hole) and two shops sufficient to serve its few hundred inhabitants.

Dean Hole's father, also called Samuel, was born at Caunton Grange, now the home of the only surviving member of the Hole family, Mrs. John Hole, who is involved locally with the National Gardens Scheme and herself maintains a fine garden, to be made open to the public on dates to be decided.

in the greenhouse and the store since then; I have won prizes of gold and cups of silver, but I have never exhibited nor seen others exhibit anything half so precious as that . . . no colour which could compare with its splendid crimson flowers.'

If the beauty of the salvia was a revelation to him, then his subsequent appreciation of the beauty of the rose was a complete conversion: 'Sauntering in the garden one summer's evening with cigar and book, and looking up from the latter during one of those vacant moods in which the mind, like the jolly young waterman, is absorbed in "thinking about nothing at all", my eyes rested on a rose . . .' The rose was *R. d'Aguesseau* (gallica). Next day he returned to the garden carrying instead of a cigar, a copy of the classic book (in 1844 just out) *The Rose Amateur's*

One section of the garden at Caunton Grange where Dean Hole was born and which is open to the public; the large floribunda rose is 'Chinatown'.

Dean Hole's grandfather (again called Samuel) sired fifteen children, and, wisely, Samuel II decided to go off on his own to Manchester to make his fortune by 'putting the spots in cotton', rather than compete for the family farm. Samuel Reynolds Hole was born there in 1819, but when he was but a few months old his father returned to Caunton, a rich man, and took up residence at Caunton Manor, which had been built about nineteen years earlier and lies almost the same distance west of the village church as the Grange lies east. Here Samuel Reynolds Hole lived as boy, curate, vicar and landowner, until he became Dean of Rochester in 1887.

He composed poetry from the age of ten and, while still at school, had one of his poems, 'The Death of William the Fourth', published in *The Nottingham Journal*. At around the same time he bought his first plant, a salvia, from the nurseries near to his school, for sixpence:

'I have grown and shown a multitude of specimens

Rosa 'Reynolds Hole', a lasting memorial to the father of our National Rose Society.

Guide, by the arch-rosarian, Rivers. Never again, declared Hole, would he wander 'flowerless through a flowery world'. When later he met the book's author, he was offered this advice: 'You may, you must, lose your present enjoyment of recreations, which require physical strength, and power of endurance, but you will never lose your delight of the garden.'

'I have fulfilled his prophecy,' Dean Hole later claimed, 'and, more than that, I regard the success which I have had in my humble but hasty efforts to persuade others to believe in this doctrine, with a gratitude which I cannot express, as the best work which I have been permitted to do.'

Much of Dean Hole's later writing carries the theme of 'gardening as character reform', as here in an excerpt from his own book, *Our Gardens*:

'The enjoyments of a garden being so manifold and continuous, bringing brightness to the home, health to the body, and happiness to the mind, it is for us, who have proved them, whose daily lives are made more cheerful by their influence, out of our gratitude and our goodwill, to invite and to instruct others, that they may share our joy. There is great need of such persuasion.'

Here is the nineteenth-century moral reformer, the 'Saul' whose personal conversion provided the motivation for what he described as 'his best work', and his father, master of the Manor, was ever understanding of the zeal of this gardening curate:

Rosa banksiae. 'As with smitten bachelor and steadfast mate the lady of his love is lovely ever, so to the true rose-grower must the rose-tree be always a thing of beauty.'

'My good old father, whose delight was in agriculture, calmly watched not only the transformation of his garden but the robbery of his farm with a quaint gravity and kindly satire, that, not doubting for a moment the lucrative wisdom of applying the best manure in unlimited quantities to the common hedgerow briar, he ventured nevertheless to express his hope that I would leave a *little* for the wheat.'

Dean Hole does not fit comfortably into the popularly held image of the country parson anaesthetising himself against the horrors of mid-nineteenth-century city life by burying his head in the bosom of nature. On the contrary, he was noted for his inner city missionary work and in 1875 given due recognition for it by the Bishop of Lincoln, Christopher Wordsworth, nephew of the poet, when he made him Canon of Lincoln Cathedral. Here Hole recalls his experience during a mission to London's East End, at a period in our history when poverty and overcrowding created appalling statistics of crime, disease and infant death (over half the deaths in London in 1839 were of children under ten years of age). 'I have just returned from a ten-days' Mission in East London. The amount of sin and misery is appalling. Such scenes as make the heart bleed. Large families crowded in a small room. Three children in a bed, two of them sick, one *dead*. The little corpse taken out at night, and put on the floor to make room for the parents! A husband brought home drowned – the wife takes off his boots and pawns them for drink!'

If some of Hole's gardening writing seems overly

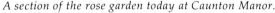

A section of the rose garden today at Caunton Manor.

evangelical, even melodramatic today, this is as much due to the different context in which we now judge it, as it is to the driving force of the man's character and his genuine conviction that the theology of God the Creator, God in nature, was the way to salvation:

'Yes my dear friends, I can assure you that I have slept the same placid, I might say porcine, slumbers, which possess you now; and in the same condition of profound ignorance have dreamed, as you are dreaming, that I had all knowledge. Hence my compassion for your sad estate, and my gratitude for the bright awaking which delivered me from darkness, and which, without diminishing any other enjoyments, conferred upon me the sweetest and the surest of them all. Let me earnestly invite you to "Shake off dull sloth, and early rise" to see and share this happiness, to apprehend the beauty which surrounds you, the grandeur, the order, the exquisite perfection, from the giant sequoia to the tiny lichen, from the cedar which is in Lebanon even to the hyssop which springeth out of the wall. You have only to search until you have found some single flower which attracts and absorbs your admiration, and that thing of beauty shall be your joy for ever. You will have entered a land which is the glory of all land, araby the blest, which has no boundaries . . . My own conversion came from a flower, which I shall never forget, more than half a century ago; and I know several instances in which the perusal of a book, the sight of a neighbour's garden, a visit to a floral exhibition, have transformed indifference into zeal.'

On his deathbed, Bishop Wordsworth, who had become a firm friend as well as an admirer, sent this message to Dean Hole: 'Tell him who is so fond of flowers, that no bed in the Garden of the soul is so beautiful as the bed of sickness and of death, on which the penitent seems to be in the presence of the Gardener . . . Tell him that these thoughts may give him a subject for a sermon.'

When Dean Hole began growing roses at Caunton, there were no societies, nurseries, shows, exhibitions or any means by which the rose was considered independently of the general flower garden. Indeed, the 'quaint gravity and kindly satire' in which old Samuel held his son's new passion arose precisely because the bush roses he cultivated with such care were then considered common hedgrow plants. Dean Hole set about changing this situation with characteristic vigour: 'Our warfare in those days was mere skirmishing,' he said later of his efforts and those of other early rosarians. 'We were only a contingent of Flora's army – the rose was but an item

The climbing rose, 'Dortmund', at Caunton Grange.

of the general flower-show. We were never called to the front . . .'

Travelling all over the country looking at roses and reading all he could find written about them, Dean Hole accumulated information, knowledge and important personal contacts in the world of horticulture. At the same time he built his own uniquely impressive collection, which eventually numbered nearly 5,000 specimens, most of which he planted in the walled garden at the end of the fountain walk at Caunton Manor, though his favourite climbing rose, 'Gloire de Dijon', was reserved for the chancel wall of the village church.

Finally, with his band of rosarians newly gathered from all over the country, he launched the first national rose show at St. James's Hall in London in July, 1858. The delicious scent of this first ever gathering of prize roses provided visitors to the show with a welcome contrast (noted at the time) to the stench and squalor of the nearby river Thames (the main water supply to the city and source of so much of its disease).

The show was a grand success, and one can imagine how much it owed to the spirit of its instigator. Eleven years later he crowned his reputation as both author and rosarian with the publication of *A Book About Roses*, written 'as Bassuet preached, *"sans etude, familierement de l'abondance du coeur".'* There are many stories about his wit and of the encouragement he lent to amateur growers at the many exhibitions over which he was frequently called to preside. On one occasion he was overheard likening the progress of one exhibitor to that of George III when he was learning the fiddle: 'The King had asked his master – the celebrated Viotti – what he thought of his pupil,' confided the Dean, 'and received, with a profound bow and courtly smile, the following reply: "Sire there are three

Above, the walled garden where he amassed his collection of nearly 5,000 roses.

Dean Hole's favourite rose, 'Gloire de Dijon'.

classes of violinists – those who cannot play at all, those who play badly, and those who play well. Your Majesty is now commencing to enter upon the second of these classes."'

His advice about growing roses, practical and succinct, holds as good for growers today: 'Let them be planted in the best place and in the best soil available, avoiding drip [from trees] and roots. Let them be manured in the winter and mulched in the spring. In the summer months let them be well watered below and well syringed above, two or three times a week. Let grubs and aphids be removed, and sulphur, or soot, or soap-and-water be applied as soon as mildew shows itself.'

Above all, Dean Hole advocated friendship between lovers of flowers and gardens, that they share their plants and ideas, and that they really love their roses: 'As with smitten bachelor or steadfast mate the lady of his love is lovely ever, so to the true rose-grower must the rose-tree be always a thing of beauty. To others when its flowers have faded it may be worthless as a hedgerow thorn! To him, in every phase, it is precious.'

St. Mary's, Portsea

Mr. Jock Macdonald

'Nobody owns a garden. A millionaire can buy all the land, but nobody can own its plants. What are you going to do when you move, take them with you? No, nobody owns a garden. Everybody that sees it – the garden becomes part of their memories. "That's a nice plant," they'll say, "I'll remember that plant." And they do; they'll remember it for years.'

Up until the eighteenth century, the parish of St. Mary's consisted of a tiny community outside the walls of the city of Portsmouth, sustaining itself by agriculture and fishing. But by the middle of the nineteenth century the spread of the Industrial Revolution (in particular the transition of the Navy from sail to steam with the attendant growth of the dockyard) had turned Portsea Island into a densely populated sea port. Today, great concrete routes loop round traffic islands into the city, a pulsating monster that wakens to the hiss of disc brakes and the escalating roar of engines straining through their gears.

Since 1895, St. Mary's has been a proving ground for some of the Church's most eminent men, producing more than a handful of Bishops, two Archbishops of York, and one Archbishop of Canterbury (Cosmo Gordon Lang). The church itself, built in 1889 by Canon Edgar Jacob on the site of its dark and dismal predecessor, is impressive: the tower is 165 feet high; the nave 123 feet long, 40 feet wide and 78 feet high; and the total external length is 210 feet – more the dimensions of a small cathedral than a parish church, and with seating for almost two thousand people.

Under Lang (1896 to 1901) the number of assistant curates rose to sixteen, which gives an idea of the size and business of the parish. Today, its incumbent, the Revd. Canon J. M. Brotherton manages with four. An unlikely situation, one might think, to foster a vicarage garden as splendid as this; and therein lies its extraordinary story.

Twenty years ago a dockyard worker, Jock Macdonald, stopped by and offered his services to cut the grass. At that time the garden was little more than a field; there was a mulberry tree near the house, but otherwise it was between 1 and 2 acres of grass and brambles. It was agreed with the incumbent that he should come and work in the garden for about six hours a week, cutting the grass and, as Jock puts it, 'getting everything down. Then, after about six months when I'd got the grass down, and so on, I said to the vicar's wife, "How about if I made a garden?" She said, "Do what you like!" And since then I have. I come and go when I like and do what I like.

'The first thing was to get some trees in because it was an even bigger garden than today. I didn't know a lot about gardening so I sent away for some catalogues where I found all these descriptions of trees: I found out about magnolias, and now I have six different ones here. Then I found out about conifers, and I've got about seventy of those. Next I found out about gleditsias . . . You see, I'd go mad on things, and then one day I thought, Roses! Fill up with great tall roses that'll spread like mad. So I got "Chinatown", "Queen Elizabeth", "Lavender Lassie", "Frank Naylor", "Iceberg", "Fountain", "Compassion", all climbers and shrub roses, all climbing over themselves. I've got between 250 and 300 roses now. Then I went mad on flowering cherries and got about six of them. Then I found out about flowering shrubs, and in each of the flowering shrubs I put a clematis. I've got about forty or fifty clematis altogether, and a Canadian lilac.'

Jock Macdonald grows literally thousands of plants

Rosa 'Paul's Scarlet' and Clematis 'Hagley Hybrid'.

Rosa 'Iceberg'.

in the vicarage garden at St. Mary's, and although he likes you to think that it's all as simple as sending off for a few catalogues and ordering the plants that take your fancy ('then just wap 'em in'), his is not a garden without a plan, albeit one that has developed over time, and as a visit establishes beyond all doubt, the colour combinations and condition of his plants are stunning and vibrant respectively.

On a sizzling hot day in July, armed only with a general address, and the knowledge that the garden had a large number of roses, we joined the stream of metal flowing down Fratton road towards the centre of the old 'working' town. We got out of the car at the Church, and glanced around for a clue as to the whereabouts of the vicarage. Observing a great surf of 'Iceberg' froth above a tall, brick garden wall across the churchyard, we made our way, rightly, to the vicarage garden gate. Once inside, the noise of traffic almost entirely disappears and the visitor is enveloped in the stillness, colours and smells of one man's inspired floral vision.

To begin with those mounds of climbing and bush roses give a sense of the cottage garden – a tangle of plants which he keeps in healthy accord rather than aggressive tension, an effect he has recalled from his

grandmother's garden which he knew as a boy. 'Felicia' and 'Pink Perpétue', 'Iceberg' and 'Compassion' shower their petals on the path below, a wooden bench inviting you to indulge the senses longer. Little vistas provide the only means to see the rest of the garden; for the moment we are confined to a rose passage, 4 foot wide. To its left he has created a

Now and then little vistas encourage the visitor to explore the garden further.

'Iceberg' and 'Compassion' in perfect harmony.

Campanula and Iceland poppy.

bird sanctuary. 'I filled it up with stinging nettles, clematis and honeysuckle, and climbing roses and shrubs ('Spanish Beauty' and 'Danse de Feu') to attract the butterflies. The birds love the shrubs to build their nests, and only I am allowed in here.

When he first began his garden plan Jock took his sons across the cratered landscape of bombed-out Portsmouth (the naval port had been a magnet for Hitler's bombs), looking for stones. 'Concrete and bricks wouldn't do, they wouldn't match the garden. We were after granite blocks, upside-down gutters and so on.' Many of these stones still mark the limits of his beds, partly to hold copious autumn levels of compost and leafmould, but also to help retain moisture in the soil. 'Haven't you noticed that when you lift a stone it's almost always damp?' He tells a story about a pilot who flew across the desert and peering out of his craft noticed what appeared to be blobs on the landscape, roughly equidistant apart. When he returned on foot to find out what they were

Lilium 'Royal Gold' and Lonicera 'Early Archangel'.

The patio is built from old, butcher's slabs and dressing-table tops. Jock has planted it with campanulas, fuchsias and penstemon, against a background of Juniperus 'Pfitzeriana', J. 'Columnaris Glauca', and, of course, a rose – R. 'Parkdirektor Riggers'.

The bog garden.

Rosa 'Elizabeth of Glamis'.

he found small piles of stones under which, many years before, seeds had been sown to give colour to the scorched soil.

The stone moving, he recalls, was the hardest work in building the garden. The image of Jock and his sons silhouetted against the sky scouring a devastated landscape is a powerful one – 'There were bushes of buddleia sprouting up soon after the bombs; amazing how quickly life returns,' – but what really strikes you is the contrast between physical achievement (no doubt managed through years of physical effort as a dockyard shift worker, seven days a week, fifty weeks a year, year in, year out), and the sensitivity with which he has created this garden.

Other features of the garden include a bog garden with *Ligularia dentata* 'Desdemona', *Lobelia cardinalis*, primulas, and red, white and pink astilbes, and island beds of conifers and tree and dwarf heathers, the inspiration of Blooms of Bressingham's Adrian Bloom. Jock travels wherever he can find good nurseries: 'Nurserymen are just about the most honest people going. I find the best of them, the people who get their hands dirty and really know

A trellis of roses and clematis changes the mood between a lawn plotted with island beds and a cottage garden beyond.

what they are doing, and pick up what I need. Every year I go over to Ventnor on the Isle of Wight – to the Shute nursery. The first time I went, I bought all these trees and I said I'm not going to take them, you're going to have to bring them over. The woman there, she said, "I only come over to the mainland once a year!" So I said, never mind, when you come, bring them. And she did.'

It took a while to realise that Jock pays for the plants in the garden, and now he tells me that this has always been the case. 'I took early retirement – at 62 – to concentrate on this garden. I wouldn't have retired if I hadn't had this. I've made other gardens, but they were for money. This is for me – this is the best. I buy the plants. I say what goes in. I pulls them out. I like to see it; it gives me great pleasure, though sometimes I'm disappointed with it.'.

How does he feel about it right now? 'I think you can say you've got your garden right when things come up which you haven't sown but you're glad to see. It's coming on; it's not at its best yet – three or four years' time, if I live that long.'

Island bed of conifers and heathers, the golden Thuja occidentalis 'Rheingold' making useful contrast in any such grouping.

THE GARDEN AT
Lis Escop

Bishop Joseph Wellington Hunkin

'A country parson without some knowledge of plants is surely as incomplete as a country parsonage without a garden.'

Truro Cathedral from the garden at Lis Escop.

Joseph Wellington Hunkin, the first Cornish Bishop of Truro, was born into a family of Methodists living but a walk away from the newly built ecclesiastic pile.

The Hunkins were fairly widely known locally, for although Joseph's father was only a coal merchant, he was also a preacher and saver of souls, given to singing hymns on street corners and falling to his knees in public prayer, his clean white handkerchief sometimes substituting for a hassock. Joseph's mother, less flamboyant, was the product of a strictly disciplined, academic upbringing, a background

which helped form the foundations of her son's later, brilliant academic record. If Mrs. Hunkin's somewhat starchy approach would not appeal to everyone it certainly didn't serve to impede her son's affection, on the contrary Joseph adored her.

Ironically, the boy reacted to his father's style of evangelism by becoming an Anglican, but in contrast to many other Methodist converts he did not at any point in his life swing towards the ritualism and mystery of High Church Anglicanism. Perhaps because of the example of his mother, he retained throughout his life a deep-seated aversion to all expressions of emotionalism in religion. This is of interest in the present context because his appointment to Truro ran counter to the Cornish diocesan trend towards High Anglicanism, and Hunkin met opposition from within, particularly over his views about the Reservation of the Sacrament in Cornish churches. Yet, and in spite of disagreement with some of them, his churchmen loved him.

Of course, they loved him despite their differences because he was a Cornishman through and through, and they loved him, too, because his reputation as first World War hero, scholar and eminent churchman, brought respect for all Cornwall from far-off places. But his real strength was that his brilliance and courage was combined with an extraordinary facility for *communication* at all levels; and this was greatly enhanced in this rural community by his love of gardening. As Alan Dunstan points out in his biography, *Cornish Bishop*, gardening became the means by which Joseph Hunkin's presence was carried deep into the fabric of Cornish life.

At the time of his consecration, Hunkin had scarcely done a day's gardening in his life. Yet, incredibly, within ten years he had become an international authority on trees and shrubs.

In this extraordinarily speedy education Canon A.T. Boscawen (see *The Garden at Ludgvan*) played a crucial role. In Boscawen's 'sympathetic co-operation with Nature' Hunkin perceived an 'inspiration' for both clergy and laity. And it was to Boscawen that he gives credit for the earliest plantings at Lis Escop which became his episcopal home – 'He came to my assistance at once. We planted a dozen *Pinus insignis* for increased shelter, and he gave me a number of beautiful things, such as *Lapageria rosea, Daphne japonica* . . . *Acacia armata*, and two or three leptospermums.'

Later Bishop Hunkin became the author of numerous, wide-ranging articles and practical gardening books, but frequently it was the gardens of his diocese that provided the subject matter for his regular column in the church magazine of the day, the *Guardian*. There, sound practical advice was always enlivened by anecdote and keen observation, and he displayed a sensitivty to the natural beauty of his diocese which captured the hearts of his people:

'Spring, the young bride of the year, chooses always a white wedding. Distinguished guests like camellias, magnolias or rhododenrons, are allowed pink or red, and late-comers like the bluebells, some other colour; but the bride herself is in shining white, with a bouquet of soft yellow.

'This year the season has been early and, thanks to mild and dry weather, flowers of every sort have

Gardening became the means by which Bishop Hunkin's presence was carried deep into the fabric of Cornish life.

been abundant. Within a week of Lady Day, sheets of white blackthorn have been lighting up the hedgerows: very common and familiar, but how beautiful! Chiming in with them along the lanes are the frequent clumps of stitchwort, each frail white flower nodding its head at every breath of wind.'

Today Lis Escop remains in Church hands. The Bishop's many rhododendrons, azalias, camellias, and other green and flowering shrubs provide a marvellously tranquil garden of meditation for the nuns of the Convent of the Community of the Epiphany. With permission of the Community we viewed the grounds in the company of Bishop Hunkin's first gardener, Mr. Blakey, now some ten years retired. Mr. Blakey recalls what a mess Lis Escop had been when Hunkin arrived and that his first question had been – '"How long will it take to make a garden?". I told him that the first five years would be spent clearing and planting.'

Mr. Blakey would be briefed once a month: 'I'd go into his study at about seven o'clock in the evening and I would often still be there at eleven talking about shrubs and what the ground wanted. He mapped it all out and suggested plants. People who knew of his interest would send him seeds or new

A fine group of deciduous azalea hybrids

specimens – there was a doctor who used to give him little boxes of seeds and other plants come from all over the place.' Pointing to two huge *Pinus Radiata*, he says – 'These we grew from seed. I remember once that the Bishop was preaching at Gulval. Would I like to come, he says: there are some young enbothriums growing in the churchyard, while I'm in church you could dig 'em up!'

The place that plants occupied in Joseph Hunkin's day-to-day life and work is charmingly illustrated by his own description of Christmas 1945, written with reference to the service of Nine Lessons and Carols that had been drawn up for the Cathedral by Truro's first Bishop, Edward White Benson:

'Instead of Christmas cards, I gave the boys of the choir an apple each from the best apple tree in Lis Escop garden, and to the men I presented button-holes, also from the garden. Next morning on the breakfast table there were button-holes for the whole household. Staff and family, ten souls in all, break-

Two huge Pinus radiata, the correct nomenclature for P. insignis, which were grown from seed, perhaps the product of collaboration between Bishop Hunkin and Canon Boscawen.

Rhododendron 'Dr. A.W. Endtz' against an embothrium, the Chilean Fire Bush.

Rosy white flowers of Magnolia x soulangiana 'Nigra', a perfect foil for the gold berberis and yellow broom.

fasted together, and we all wore button-holes of the same pattern. Each was built on a sprig of Skimmia with its dark shining green leaves and bright red holly-like berries. To this were added a couple of pieces of rich purple heath, and one of winter sweet for fragrance, with its yellow florets on the bare twig.

Christmas Day was mild and bright, and after we had returned from Morning Prayer my wife and I walked round the garden and counted the shrubs which were in considerable flower. There were just over two dozen . . . The walk was a good preparation for turkey and Christmas pudding, and the family giving of presents around the log fire in the dining hall, the singing of carols by the whole household, and finally a charade "featuring" national and local celebrities . . . the most care-free Christmas for many years.'

As a sort of climax to his pastoral mission, Bishop Hunkin instigated a project, a sort of living memorial in the shape of a gift of some first-class shrubs and trees to each of the parishes in his diocese. At Lis Escop, 'he raised and collected a number of plants for this purpose,' wrote W. Arnold-Foster, in 1951, 'and had distributed a few of them before his sudden death.' Hunkin's project survived his unfortunate death in an anaesthetist's chair in a dentist's surgery in London, thanks to the efforts of Arnold-Foster himself who succeeded him as Chairman of the Cornwall Branch of the Council for the Preservation of Rural England. Each incumbent was sent a letter asking whether such a memorial gift would be acceptable, what kind of plant would be preferred and whether the intended site was exposed, sheltered, or 'medium'. Every church, rather than just every parish as first intended, was covered by the scheme and over 250 plants were eventually despatched.

THE GARDEN AT

Diss

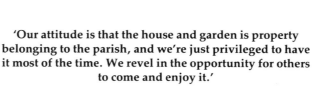

The Reverend and Mrs. Gordon James

'Our attitude is that the house and garden is property belonging to the parish, and we're just privileged to have it most of the time. We revel in the opportunity for others to come and enjoy it.'

The tradition of English vicarage and rectory gardening held firm during the war years. Mrs. Helen Cook recalls that in the rectory at Diss, in Norfolk, where her father was incumbent from 1940 to 1952, the feeling of sharing the property was never stronger. 'I found a letter last night in which my father wrote that the grass was growing into a field – he was desperate because there were the usual scouts' and cubs' evenings and so on, and every fortnight during the war we had fruit and vegetable shows to encourage people to grow things ('Dig for Victory'), yet he couldn't get permission for two gallons of petrol for his mower. He applied and waited and waited, and when finally permission came they gave him enough to mow from Land's End to John O' Groats! But the letter brought to mind how in those days the rectory was always crowded with people. There was a long room on the first floor given over to evacuees and we even had them in the attic. People would

be bombed out of London and come away as far as Diss, thinking themselves safe and that someone would put them up. At one stage at the end of the war we had four different families under this roof, waiting for somewhere to live.

'The rectory was one house then, and included the beamed part which is now the rectory cottage. The garden was much bigger too, and we had a gardener to look after it. There was a tennis court, lots of apple trees, and I remember a vine in the greenhouse where houses are built now. But the thing we all loved so much was the old mulberry tree – still there at the top of the garden, but propped up now. I remember it more the size of the chestnut (though perhaps it wasn't quite so tall) – it would literally drip mulberries on us.'

We were sat looking out at the lovely garden through the long drawing room bay windows of this seventeenth-century rectory house. But whatever we could see was a pale reflection of Helen's view: 'The man who became my husband was a chaplain in the Derbyshire Yeomanry then. Like so many others he had come to Diss to find somewhere to stay, and naturally called to see the rector first to ask his advice. My father said, "Well, why don't you come here, my daughter's away at College, there's one room at least." And that was the beginning of everything for me. It was in this room that we first met; it was in this room that he proposed; it was in this room that we had our wedding reception . . . but that's quite another story.'

John Betjeman once described Diss as his favourite Norfolk town, and Mount Street itself, where the rectory stands, as the most unspoiled in any English town. Thankfully it is too compact a town to have allowed drastic change since that time, and Mount Street now comprises the Diss Conservation area. The whole rectory property, including stables and outhouses, is listed.

The house, Elizabethan in origin, is a wattle and daub property with no more thickness to its main walls than the frames of its ancient windows. Changes have been made to house and garden for economy's sake, as Helen pointed out, but the garden still occupies an acre and the house is spacious enough. The property must have posed something of a problem to a Church Authority that has left only one other old rectory property extant in the whole of South Norfolk. Its present rector, the Revd. Gordon James, and his wife arrived in Diss seven years ago from a small, modern house with virgin garden in Weston Longville. Gordon was the first incumbent of that Norfolk parish not to have enjoyed the great Georgian rectory in which James Woodford wrote *The Diary of a Country Parson* (see *Introduction*). He hopes that this time they may be spared: 'They certainly would like to get rid of this as a rectory, but I gather that they are beginning to think that the whole policy of dissolution is mistaken. Twenty years ago they were building all the new, 'trouble-free' properties, but today they are finding that they're actually jolly expensive: they are just not built to the substantial standards of many old properties. There may be a re-think.'

The garden is pleasantly and practically planned

The mulberry tree still staggers on, even surviving with minimal damage that bad storm in October '87.

Looking across the herb and gladioli garden towards the church; the honeysuckle is L. x americana.

Conifers either side of a flight of steps leading up to the rose garden help focus the garden's main view which is visible from all of the rectory's east-side windows. Among roses climbing over a pergola are 'New Dawn' and 'Albertine' through which Lonicera caprifolium grows.

by the rector and his wife, stunning use having been made of the nearby Blooms of Bressingham's specialism in conifers and heathers – very aptly too, for Mrs. James' Christian name is Erica.

It comprises a large lawn of irregular shape, bounded on the the East side by the rectory house. In front stands a small pool and border bed – hostas, hellebores, Easter lilies, bulbs, potentilla with vinca growing round about, nothing so tall that the view up the garden from the drawing room bay window is obscured. The south-side border bed includes an acer, weigela, a variegated privet shrub, alchemilla, a deep red honeysuckle riding on a rose, polyanthus, fritillaries, lily of the valley, ceanothus, euonymus, more hellebores, Solomon's Seal (*Polygonatum multi-*

A perfect symbiosis of formal and wilder forms – a bank of dwarf and prostrate conifers and heathers including Erica carnea 'Foxhollow' (yellow), E. c. 'Springwood' (white), E. x darleyensis, Lavandula officinalis, Juniperus x media 'Old Gold' (bottom left), violas, Festuca glauca (a useful edging plant), aubrieta and saxifrage.

florum), sedums, aquilegia, mahonia, saxifrage, and so on, and a favourite background material for the arrangements that Mrs. James enjoys both for fun and competition: elephant's ears (*Bergenia spp.*).

A path leads behind this border to a rectangular herb garden offering mint, orange and lemon flavoured herbs, sage, chives, rosemary, etc., a bed of gladioli (the rector's passion) tucked carefully out of the way for cutting purposes, and a clear view of the thirteenth-century church tower across an ancient wall clothed with montana.

Both north and west sides of the garden are dominated by specimen trees, the northern side being their pride and joy in spring when beneath a row of ancient beech appear, in unbroken succession, aconites, scillas, crocus, hyacinths, daffodils, and finally bluebells.

On the west we find the tallest tree in the world – not this actual specimen of *Sequoia sempervirens* since, it is explained, the Californian redwood never grows as well outside its natural climate. But it's a mighty tree nonetheless, and a well-known landmark

Castanea mollissima, the Chinese chestnut.

The bright colours and perfect 'honeycomb' form of the Pompon dahlia provide interest from early August until the first frosts, and the flower is of course ideal for indoor floral arrangments.

round about. In its shade and certainly as old – possibly a hundred years or more – staggers Helen's precious mulberry, which despite its geriatric appearance is still, the rector assures us, prolifically fruitful.

In front lies the garden's major focal area, visible quite intentionally from all the rectory's east-side windows: first a rose garden, some 8 or so feet above the level of the lawn and arranged around a central sundial. Helen remembers this as being quite similar in her day, though then the roses gave way to a grassy slope leading down to the lawn. Today Gordon and Erica have transformed the slope into a marvellously shaped bed of conifers and heathers, occasionally interspersed with specimen hostas and hedging lavender, dwarf broom and potentilla, formal and wilder plant forms which somehow combine to create a perfect symbiosis and give a natural feel to a type of low-maintenance planting which so often looks soullessly artificial. From the end of June the roses rise above this bed and complete the picture – the orchestra pit (the heathers) and the performers' stage (the rose garden) being Gordon's image of their garden's set piece.

As we watch the drama in progress, the eye is drawn to the left of the feature bed to Gordon's favourite tree, *Castanea mollissima*, the Chinese chestnut, which provides perfect dappled shade for 'the damp corner', and a surprising variety of colour: trollius, astilbes, euphorbias, cotoneaster and philadelphus, as well as ferns.

North-west of the garden lies a part of the garden that is hidden from view from the house. An herbaceous bed of old-fashioned plants – delphiniums, polygonum, hemerocallis and *Achillea ptarmica* 'The Pearl', good for cutting (as is so much else in Erica's beds) – is framed by an ancient rose climbing

up the stump of an old tree, and blackberries and plums against an old brick wall, separated from the bed by a tiny path. Further west are the fruit and vegetable garden and a serious cutting bed for dahlias and gladioli, which produces volumes during the summer for church, rectory, and competition. The edible garden offers all the usual soft and tree fruit and vegetables, and Erica only ever needs to buy for variety (and the occasional cauliflower, which she admits to finding difficult). They tend not to spray, due to lack of time more than anything else but also because Erica puts her faith in garden hygiene as the best protection against disease: 'I'm a great one for clearing up waste and diseased leaves, burning the rubbish and keeping it out of the compost heaps. I believe that trying to keep the garden in control is the best preventive medicine.'

Situated right in the town, just a few steps from the bustle of Diss, this garden immediately infuses the visitor with a sense of peace. The effect has yet to be lost on Gordon and Erica in the six years they have been there. 'And we are pleased to encourage its use as much as we can,' the Rector adds. 'We have the

The north-west 'cottage' border includes echinops, delphiniums, Lysimachia punctata, physalis, Solidago 'Golden Thumb', tradescantia, saxifrage, Achillea 'The Pearl', Acanthus spinosus, armeria (thrift) and pinks.

youth group over, parish barbecues, garden parties, Mother's Union gatherings and so on. Our attitude is that the house and garden is property belonging to the parish, and we're just privileged to have it most of the time. We revel in the opportunity for others to come and enjoy it.'

A colourful, 'damp' corner. In front of the Chinese chestnut, (back row, left to right) Cotoneaster horizontalis, Astilbe 'Venus', a hardy fern, Hosta sieboldiana 'Elegans', (middle) Pulmonaria saccharata 'Margery Fish', Monarda 'Cambridge Scarlet', (front) Alchemilla mollis and trollius.

THE GARDEN AT

Clun

The Reverend and Mrs. Ernest Buckley

'After two or three years (when we felt we had got the garden into shape), Ruth said, "What's the point of toiling away and nobody enjoying it except ourselves and people at the odd parish function." My first reaction was to say, "Not on your life!" . . . in fact it has worked out very well – not least to pay the quota!'

The story goes that during the Civil War, the men of Clun got so fed up watching Parliamentarians marching up and down the main street one day, and Royalists the next, that they got together to defend themselves against both! It's a small community, about eight or nine hundred people today, and its strength is that it is a community in which most of the people are related. Whenever someone has been in difficulty there have always been other members of the family to help out.

The Reverend Ernest Buckley, incumbent since 1979 and shortly to retire with his gardening wife, Ruth, to the nearby hamlet of Cluntown, relishes the

Looking across the three main flowerbeds in spring, towards the church.

closeness of the community, but like Clun's other residents he welcomes visitors to it as well. The whole area – the Clun Valley, situated on the Welsh border a few miles west of Craven Arms – is steeped in history; there are Iron Age hill forts, Norman Castles, seventeenth-century alms houses and a sixteenth-century pub where, if you stray into the public bar to the right of its entrance rather than the lounge and restaurant to the left, the spoken dialect will baffle you even before the local ale. Here, fresh produce still warm from field and forest, is rustled in by locals, passes under the hands of the Egon Ronay chef and emerges, stage left, for the delectation of an international clientele.

Visitors – summer tourists – are a feature of Clun, and most will make its ancient church (a Victorian re-build admittedly but darkly attractive and incorporating many of its original Norman parts) part of the tour. Realising this, and above all wanting to share the enjoyment it offers, Ernest Buckley agreed to open the vicarage garden to the public: 'My first reaction was to say, "Not on your life!" I think that what I was frightened of was a loss of privacy. I had visions of paragraphs in national magazines, of starting something we could never keep up. But Ruth persisted, and eventually I allowed her a very small notice on the Town Hall board. And, again, just a little notice in the church. It all developed from there and, in fact, it has worked out very well – not least to pay the quota! We put what we make into church funds.

'We really do get an enormous number of visitors to the church and the garden is simply a very nice little spot to spend another pleasant hour of your holiday.'

Then in the summer of 1984 things began to take off. Ruth explains: 'There are quite a number of keen

Left: the wall bed in the lower garden in July. On the wall are spring flowering Clematis macropetala and japonica, white edging clumps of Viola cornuta alba, and yellow Welsh poppies (Meconopsis cambrica). The bed leads up a slope to the three main beds, which create wonderful flowering vistas up to the Leyland cypress or back down towards the house. Above, the centre bed in June.

gardeners around Clun and we all really went to town to create a flower festival that took everyone by surprise. Some said it was better than the festival at Bath Abbey. It took twelve months of preparation.' Inside the church they needed scaffolding to build the display, each part dedicated to telling some part of Christ's story from the nativity through the miracles, and on to the resurrection and finally, the ascension which flared up over the reredos behind the altar and up onto the East window.'

When Ruth Buckley tells you that there are a number of keen gardeners in the area one gets the impression that this is understatement, for just over the road in Church Cottage lives the horticulturalist and plant hunter, the Reverend Richard Blakeway-Phillips, sometime vicar of Little Abington in Cambridgeshire and Crawley Down in Sussex. Richard has gained sixty-six awards for plants from *The Royal Horticultural Society* including ten Cultural Commendations; he is a Gold Medallist of the Alpine Garden Society and has their Farrer Medal for the

The Apple Tree border in June (see plant list). 'In the large borders, my favourites are Campanula lactiflora, the columbines (Aquilegia spp.), the lemon yellow Anthemis tinctoria 'E.C. Buxton', the hardy geraniums and, of course, the delphiniums.

The table at the gate, where it all began.

Hepatica 'Crawley Down'.

best plant in the London Autumn Show of 1978. Among his cultivars are *Hepatica* 'Crawley Down', *Hepatica nobilis* 'Little Abington', *Iris unguicularis* 'Abington Purple' and *Galanthus* 'Clare Blakeway-Phillips', named after an elder daughter. But back to the flower festival . . .

'As well as the flowers in the church we also had teas on the lawn, and a stall which we operated for three days. Anyone not involved with the refreshments or the stall would help out with the parish exhibition in the church hall (all part of the same building complex). At that point we simultaneously opened nine other Clun gardens to the public. And it was then that we got the idea of the table at the gate.'

'We heard tell of a previous vicar's wife who would put flowers out for sale,' continues Ernest Buckley, 'so Ruth, having a surfeit of flowers from the garden began to do the same, and they sold for church funds. The table began to attract yet more visitors, and when they walked around the garden they would see something in flower which they rather liked and would say, "Oh, have you got one of these?" and

The left-hand side of the kitchen garden, tucked under the protecting arm of an old Bramley. This side includes vegetables, a nursery bed for primroses, polyanthus, and Primula denticulata, and a row of Sweet Rocket for cutting. The right-hand side is reserved for soft fruit.

gradually Ruth developed a whole garden centre.'

There must have been a carefully tended garden here for some time (though due to illness and brevity of office respectively the last two incumbents had let it go – when the Buckleys arrived, it was 'waist-high, even shoulder-high with weeds'). A cottage originally built to house a full-time gardener, still exists with a path leading from it through a gate into the vicarage, and there are the remains of a Victorian nut walk . . . and, of course, there is *The Tree*.

'It's a great big, enormous Leyland cypress, which Alan Mitchell, the tree expert, tells us has the fifth

Left: looking up the garden towards The Tree. Above, Viburnum plicatum 'Mariesii' beyond the nut walk.

biggest girth in the world and is "an unknown clone"! The long and the short of all the technicalities is that there were two others like it in Kew, which have been lost, and while Alan was here he reached up and took a spray, and carried it off to the Alice Holt forestry place, subsequently propagating it under the name of 'Clun Rectory'. We had quite a battle with him to have it called by its proper nomenclature 'Clun Vicarage'. Indeed someone sent me a cutting from the *Guardian* quite recently in which he mentioned it as 'Clun Rectory' and that it was to be found in Powys! So I wrote off at top speed and said, "*Please*, we are Clun Vicarage and we are in England," and he says he has now corrected it.'

This is a garden for plants and views, as our pictures show, but its lawn also makes a natural theatre; the church, the house and the old stable wall providing beautiful acoustics for parish productions. 'The senior citizens come once a year and stagger along in the path of the children before them, who do a concert for them. We use it a lot for children, the few that there are in Clun. There is a family service once a month and I try to plan something for them afterwards,' says Ernest. 'As often as not it's a chase round the garden. We have dragon hunts. You see the church is St. George, so the youngsters call themselves dragons and go off hunting, slaying the seven deadly sins and so on.'

Church and garden meet to form a natural theatre.

Poppies add to the colour of the main centre bed in June.

Helianthemum 'Ben Afflick'.

Selected summer plant lists for the three main flowerbeds

The Apple Tree Border
June (predominant colour, pink):
Cream lupins
Cream-coloured Goatsbeard
Veronica 'Crater Lake Blue' (royal
 blue)
Aquilegia (pink/blue)
Astrantia major (white)
A. maxima (pink)
Pink poppy
Thalictrum aquilegifolium (soft purplish
 pink)
Hardy geraniums (various)

**July (predominant colour, blue and
 cream):**
Delphiniums are the main feature at
 the back
Campanula persicifolia (blue and
 white)
Anthemis tinctoria (bright yellow)
A.t. 'E.C. Buxton' (lemon yellow)
Buphthalmum salicifolia (yellow)
Cephalaria tatarica (pale yellow
 scabious)

**August (pink and white, later
 running to yellows):**
White daisy
Sidalcea (pink)
Echinops (blue)
Phlox (mostly pink and mauve)
Blue and white scabious
Golden rod

The Main, Centre Bed
June:
Much as the Apple Tree Border except
the lupins are mostly pink and a very
striking brick-red. The colour scheme
is continued with dianthus and
poppies – pink, red, and exceptionally
dark red believed to be 'King George'.

July:
Again, delphiniums (up the centre of
the bed) and goatsbeard (in three
creamy clumps), and at the end of the
month three large clumps of *Centaurea
macrocephala*, 'whose giant yellow
thistles always intrigue visitors and
seem very little known', and a gigantic

Rosa 'Nevada' at the head of the third main border.

clump of *Campanula lactiflora* (white).
August planting is similar to the
Apple Tree border.

The Third Border
This border running parallel to the
other two main flowerbeds is a mixed
bed of shrubs and herbaceous
perennials, and includes:

Spiraea x arguta
S. 'Anthony Waterer'
Many euphorbias
Hellebores Laburnum
Campanula lactiflora (deep blue)
Various hypericum
Roses on pillars – 'Golden Showers',
 'Frensham', 'New Dawn'
Mahonia 'Charity'

Deutzia
Weigela
Hardy geraniums
Lamium 'Beacon Silver'
. . .and violas in every nook and
cranny, Mrs. Buckley's favourite plant.

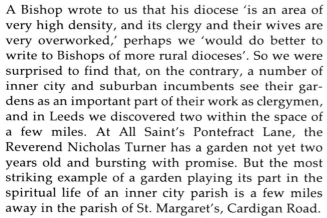

THE·GARDEN AT
St Margaret's, Leeds

The Reverend Elizabeth M. Baxter

'We see our ministry as being the building up of relationships and representing Christ in the community. The church, the vicarage and the garden are the hub.'

A Bishop wrote to us that his diocese 'is an area of very high density, and its clergy and their wives are very overworked,' perhaps we 'would do better to write to Bishops of more rural dioceses'. So we were surprised to find that, on the contrary, a number of inner city and suburban incumbents see their gardens as an important part of their work as clergymen, and in Leeds we discovered two within the space of a few miles. At All Saint's Pontefract Lane, the Reverend Nicholas Turner has a garden not yet two years old and bursting with promise. But the most striking example of a garden playing its part in the spiritual life of an inner city parish is a few miles away in the parish of St. Margaret's, Cardigan Road.

St. Margaret's is dominated by rows of back-to-back houses strung together by lines of drying saris across its barren streets. A large Asian contingent is complemented by a fair-sized student body (from the nearby university) renting often poor but relatively expensive bed-sits in what were once the impressively spacious detatched homes of Victorian industrialists. In smaller semi-detached houses there's a smattering of first-time house buyers who can afford nothing better but will move as soon as they can, together with a number of 'extended' white families where daughter has married or moved in with someone down the road from Mum, and auntie lives just round the corner.

The social picture is one of some poverty alongside increasing wealth – the fruits of an enterprising immigrant population. There are many one-parent families among the white people, a statistic not entirely separate from those of child abuse (which are among the worst in the country), in that boyfriends of young single mothers pass in and out of the area not always with their childrens' best interests at heart. There is loneliness, especially

'As a matter of serious theology, I have set about creating a proper vicarage garden as a sign of God the Creator,' said Nicholas Turner ratifying Forbes Watson's theme (see The Garden at Bitton) that 'plants have more than a sensuous value, for the imagination discovers that they are but a symbolic language.'

among Moslem women who still don't speak English and who are kept at home by their more worldly men; and there is violence, alcoholism, and depression. 'A lot of our work is of a reconciling nature (forgiveness has been very much a focus of our ministry),' explains one of St. Margaret's pastoral caretakers.

As if the situation wasn't sufficiently confused, St. Margaret's has recently been amalgamated with the neighbouring parish of All Hallows up the hill, a parish where the back-to-back housing has been demolished and a brand new vicarage and church

View across the garden at St. Margaret's. 'The garden seemed to be a trigger for the community . . . it is so important to actually see flowers, to see things that are beautiful.'

hall built, but which introduces a wholly different aspect into the cultural mosaic of the living, in the shape of a sizeable Caribbean population.

The water garden at All Saints under construction.

Conveniently, the parish priest of St. Margaret's is married to his curate, Elizabeth, who was recently made a deacon and is one of the very few women in the Anglican Church who carries the title of 'Reverend'. Together they live, not in the brand new vicarage of All Hallows, but in St. Margaret's own great rambling vicarage adjacent to the church and the old church hall. Elizabeth explains why: 'One of the things that drew us to the parish was the big house and the garden, because the kind of ministry we exercise is helped by keeping open house. They were going to get rid of it just before we came six years ago, but we rather took the line that if we were to come we would come to *this* vicarage, and in the end we won the battle and held onto it. In fact it has been agreed that as long as we are here, it will stay, but as soon as we go it'll come down or be sold off.

'The garden was a bonus right from the beginning. When we took it over it was like Sleeping Beauty's Castle – just covered with bindweed. So we got that sorted out first, and then my son bought some chickens; the chickens led to ducks, and then another son bought a goat. The Shetland pony was the family's Christmas present one year, and then other people started to give us animals: at the moment we have two little puppies that were found abandoned in an outside loo down the road; then there are the pigeons that have been hurt and brought here; rabbits that no-one wants suddenly appear and because we don't keep them in hutches they breed fairly wildly.

'The garden seemed to be a trigger for the community. You have to realise that people round here have no gardens at all. The back-to-backs have neither front nor back gardens, and I don't know whether you noticed but when you come into this parish – from either end – the trees stop! There are literally no trees in the parish at all, not a tree nor a leaf, hardly a blade of grass. Yes there are some play spaces for children, and a park just the other side of the busy main road, but by the time the alcoholics have scattered their glass around they are not safe for children.

'To begin with we planted a lot of flowers and got a vegetable patch going too (though lately many have been eaten by the animals and our present project is to enclose the animals down one end of the garden and begin re-planting). It is so important to actually see flowers, to see things that are beautiful. Very few of our people ever get the chance, the children never go to the country except on the odd school trip.'

To understand how the Baxters use their garden it is worth knowing something about their work: 'We have always been very involved with the community itself, supporting and encouraging community associations. We are planning a dispute centre in the autumn to help in reconciling personal grievances. In place of the old church hall there is soon to be a brand new community centre with workshops for the unemployed; we're working together with the council on that. There's to be another youth and community centre up at the All Hallows church hall, now that the youth training scheme is moving out, and that will be organised completely by the Church.

'We see our ministry as being the building up of relationships and representing Christ within the community. The church, the vicarage and the garden are the hub of that community.'

The garden is used for maypole dancing, barn dances, coffee mornings, teas for the summer fayre, strawberries-and-cream evenings, cheese and wine evenings, young people's barbecues, Brigade evenings, and childrens clubs. Every Sunday after Church, the congregation packs into the enormous drawing room for coffee and if it's fine the children soon spill out through the door into the garden. The Baxters encourage people to just come and sit in the garden at any time – bring a newspaper and just sit down, have a cup of tea or something, make use of it,

'The church, the vicarage and the garden are the hub of the community.'

Even in the winter, children come and feed the animals. 'For us the message of Jesus is that there is something beautiful to be found within the community, and if they can get a glimpse of that through the garden and through contact with the animals (seeing that they respond to care and love), then they are touching on something.'

and people do. Even in the winter children come to feed the animals. 'I would say that the garden has been a real bonus in the building of a family church, which is not "Churchy" but outward looking towards the community,' Elizabeth concludes. 'It is a

big place; we have got an awful lot that other people haven't got but I think it is recognised generally by the community that all of it is shared with them. For us the message of Jesus is to do with the *whole* of a person, that there is something beautiful to be found within the community, and if they can get a glimpse of that through the garden and – hopefully – through seeing a happy, loving family here, and even through contact with the animals (seeing that they respond to care and love), then they are touching on something.'

Plants and animals outside their natural habitat are, like children, totally dependent; does this fact make a woman the natural instigator of the St. Margaret's scheme? 'I don't imagine that if my husband had been here on his own things would have developed in exactly the same way, but we share our aims completely. He is as much concerned that relationships between people in the community can develop through the "hub", but he's very much involved in getting dug deep into the community. He's the one dealing with the building of the community centre, and at the back here we are hoping for a big housing development. I am more involved in the pastoral work within homes and with people who are fairly broken – he gets involved too, but I'm often the one that makes the initial contact. You see, it's a woman who is needed for this because a lot of these families are single-parent, a lot have been in 'battered wives' refuges . . . A lot of women and children, their only experience of men has been very bad . . . But, equally, we tend to work together as much as possible, as husband and wife, because it is important to show that a man and woman can actually live together happily.'

Cirencester

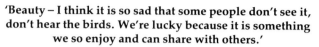

The Reverend and Mrs. John Beck

'Beauty – I think it is so sad that some people don't see it, don't hear the birds. We're lucky because it is something we so enjoy and can share with others.'

The Reverend John Beck is both priest and organist (an Oxford organ scholar), member of *The Hardy Plant Society* and, with his wife, gardener of a plantsman's paradise in Cecily Hill, Cirencester, in the County of Gloucester, which he opens to the public each year on certain days from the end of June. John Beck also raises plants for others in a nursery part of the garden, one of his most valued customers being the well-known plantswoman and author, Rosemary Verey, for her nearby garden at Barnsley.

'My love of plants dates back to my return from National Service in Egypt to "England's green and pleasant land". My next brother (I am the oldest of three) was then at horticultural college at Pershore and I used to go over there. I think that this is always the beginning of the great awakening, when you see plants supremely well grown. I would have been about 21 at that time. But we had always been taught by our father to look at things. He wasn't an expert gardener, though he had a knowledge. As a young man he had won a scholarship to the Birmingham School of Art, but he was one of nine children and even with the scholarship his parents couldn't afford to let him go. Instead he began as an apprentice with H. H. Martin's of Cheltenham, no longer extant but famous in time for some of the greatest wood carving and sculpture in the world: Martin's made the Speaker's chair in the House of Commons and the pulpit of St. Paul's Cathedral and a great number of things of that kind around the world.

'Whether it was flowers, architecture or oil paint-

View over the wall of the upper garden in early summer. The rose just beginning to show colour is the Hybrid Tea 'Oriana'. The top of the wall (used for feeding the birds in winter) is planted with various saxifrages, sedums and sempervivums.

ing my father always encouraged us to *look* at things of beauty. My earliest recollection of this relates to his work in stained glass. I must have been about 5 years old. A lovely mediaeval glass window had been taken out of a Gloucester church when it was being demolished, and the idea was to re-set it in another

suburban church on the other side of the city. He took me over there and showed me the glass and explained what he was going to do. But his biggest project was at the end of the war when the great East window of Gloucester Cathedral had to be restored and replaced. It was as big as a tennis court – the largest in the world until Coventry Cathedral was built, and very ancient, fourteenth century. So hurriedly was it taken out, however, that a lot of it smashed, and my father was given the job of piecing Humpty Dumpty together again. It was brought to his studio in Cheltenham and it took him two whole years of his life, working single-handed, a section at a time. He regarded this as the most rewarding project of his whole life.'

It was extraordinary to sit in John Beck's study talking about his father's art and then to walk through his house and into the garden to discover that what he has created is itself a sort of floral stained glass window. Though two-tiered, the lower section is a plot also about the size of a tennis court, which from June presents a mass of colour from a vast variety of hardy perennials. In Spring, before the plants have really got going, each prospective patch of colour and interest is clearly separated by curved ribs of earth and three long, straight paths which could be the stone columns of some great ecclesiastical window.

But in one sense this does John Beck an injustice, because unlike a window, his garden is a *kaleidoscope* of colour whose patterns change with the turn of time. Also, despite an apparently fairly rigid structure, the straightness of line contained in the three main paths does not in effect offend the eye, or cause a tunnel effect, because his plants conspire against it by flowing over the beds onto the paths.

The whole garden is walled, and the upper, ground-level garden belongs to Mrs. Beck, who knows exactly what she likes. 'My favourite colours are red, blue, pink and white. I like strong colours, essentially because I like positive things – like I wish our Bishops would be more positive about our faith! But I am coming round to yellows and oranges now because I also like the gentle, ethereal things – they are a reminder of the transcendental "other worldliness" that we should experience as well.'

The essence of the top garden is flowing lines, beds bounded by quite narrow, curving grass paths. There is a fine potentilla brought from Bodnant, an enormous bush of *Rosa* 'Ferdinand Pichard', which in mid-June was just forcing its reddish buds, a riot of pink and blue cranesbill washing over a rockery (different coloured flowers – black sheep of the family – providing added interest), campanulas and pop-

pies: a splendidly tall and pink plant of *Papaver orientale* 'Sultana', with a mass of white mallows in front soon to be dwarfed by the rosy-pink flowers of a *Lavatera olbia* 'Rosea'.

Through a honeysuckle archway interspersed with a rose that could be a 'Rambling Rector' or perhaps a 'Seagull' (but Mrs. Beck believes to be neither), we walk down ancient stone steps into John Beck's

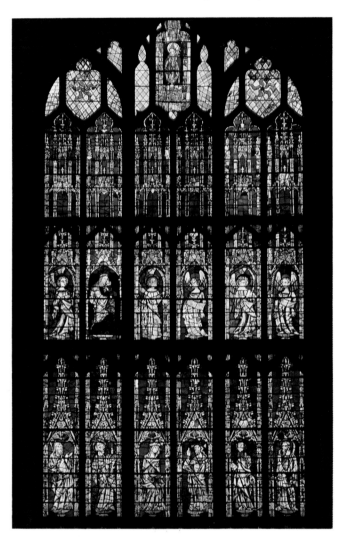

A section of the East Window at Gloucester Cathedral which John Beck's father pieced back together after the war.

garden some 15 feet below. This is by far the bigger of the two. On the immediate right lies his nursery patch. Nearby, a large arc of a bed dominated by the gnarled remains of a fallen apple tree springs to life in June with a chance combination of blue geraniums and the dashing white of a spiraea. On the first of the main strip beds, a more deliberate effect – two mounds of yellow potentilla set off by the blue shafts of

A large arc of a bed dominated by a fallen apple tree.

The effective colour combination of Spiraea nipponica 'Snow-mound' and Geranium wlassovianum.

A rose wall in the upper garden includes Rosa gallica 'Complicata', R. rugosa 'Roseraie de l'Hay', R. noisettiana 'Mme. Alfred Carrière'.

Salvia 'May Night' in between – takes prime position.
    It would be impossible to describe all of John Beck's plants. Be advised, go and see. Look one way and you will find the giant leaves of the gunnera set

Potentilla 'Elizabeth' (with Helichrysum 'Sulphur Light'), Salvia 'May Night', and a potentilla seedling. Paeonia 'Bowl of Beauty' by the wall.

In shade, Hosta crispula, Primula alpicola and P. florindae, Lilium regale, Iris sibirica 'Orientalis', and Rheum palmatum 'Atropurpureum'.

off by the purple foliage of a rheum. Look another towards roses, paeonies and clematis, or a damp, shaded area where clever use is made of form and leaf variety, or look into a sunny cottage garden corner, wildly planted with restful colour. This is a plantsman's paradise indeed, each time you walk around it you experience some new effect, partly because the beds are so arranged that at any one time you are surrounded by plants which offer a rich choice of views, and partly because of the sheer number of plants to see. 'We don't go in for repetition; we like to grow as big a variety as we can.'

Great care is taken to prepare the ground with compost and bonemeal – 'bonemeal because it is slow acting and produces a good steady growth, not rank or lush.'

Plantsmen the Becks may be, but their garden is far from a botanical experiment. 'We find gardening a great release,' John says. 'We both work very hard – I

am a bit of a "2-in-1", I do a priest's work and an organist's, which sadly means that the time we can spend out here is limited; we would love to garden to perfection.' Mrs. Beck finds the hard work in the garden a good balance – 'If you have something upsetting you, you can put your back into it. Also, its instructive. Tending difficult plants is sometimes like dealing with a difficult child in the choir, a child, say, whom you are trying to help, nurture, give that extra bit of attention to, in gardening terms "bring it on".

'From June we eat in the garden whenever we can and always work here on our day off, Thursday. Plants are natural, they are Nature – all right we planted them here, but they are simple, without Man's so-called wonderful technology. I could sit out here all day if there was the time. I think it is so sad that some people cannot see beauty – some just *don't* see it. They don't hear the birds, they've got to have

there's all that organisation and discipline there beneath the surface, they can then really concentrate on the beauty itself, something that will transcend their normal experience.'

Next door is a garden produced for a quite different effect, a sweeping lawn with elegant lines, well-placed trees, a designer garden which some days opens to the public in concert with the Becks'. On one such day Mrs. Beck was standing in for her neighbours, taking the visitors' money as they trooped into this garden after seeing her own, and two ladies came bustling by, one saying to the other, 'Oh, this is better; all that other garden had was plants!'

The Becks laugh at the memory, 'They were right! It began as chaos and ruin, but we have made a home for plants.'

John Beck's nursery garden, source of great interest among visitors on open days.

Rubble and ground elder at the bottom of the lower garden has given way to a 'wild' planting which includes Tradescantia 'Carmine Glow', Geranium pratense 'Mrs. Kendall Clerk', Geranium 'Johnson's Blue', Polygonium bistorta 'Superbum', Potentilla 'Flamenco', and Berberis thunbergii.

their transistor radios on and their noise. We are so lucky because it is something that we enjoy, and which we can share with others. Yet still people will visit the garden and come through the house and say, "Ooh, haven't you made yourself a lot of work!"

'We think that a certain naturalness, as opposed to strict formality, helps to remind us that we are not in control. Perhaps our enjoyment of the informal approach is a reaction to our attitude towards worship, because I cannot do with informal worship – we like things to be structured rather than unstructured when it comes to music and liturgy. Then again, perhaps a garden should be like a service that is well produced without being pompous: if you can do it so well that nobody *notices* that it has been deliberately well done, so that people don't feel that

St. John & St. James,
London SW9

The Reverend and Mrs. Lyle Dennen

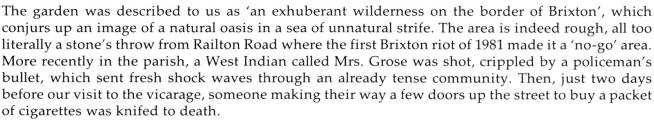

'Edward King had this vision of the church as "a garden in the city", a place of beauty that would bring beauty out of the local people. In many ways the theme of our garden is the same.'

The garden was described to us as 'an exhuberant wilderness on the border of Brixton', which conjurs up an image of a natural oasis in a sea of unnatural strife. The area is indeed rough, all too literally a stone's throw from Railton Road where the first Brixton riot of 1981 made it a 'no-go' area. More recently in the parish, a West Indian called Mrs. Grose was shot, crippled by a policeman's bullet, which sent fresh shock waves through an already tense community. Then, just two days before our visit to the vicarage, someone making their way a few doors up the street to buy a packet of cigarettes was knifed to death.

'It is a community in chaos and disorder,' agrees its incumbent, the Reverend Lyle Dennen, the result of poor planning and, worse, a paternalistic attitude on the part of the authorities, 'who have failed to understand that the community itself should have a say in the agenda.'

The basic plan is a rosary, a central circle of free-form roses off which leads a series of different rooms.

Equally, he continues, 'it is a wonderful place to live. The first thing to realise is that, living here, one doesn't see it as a problem. There is enormous variety; the mix of people is so exciting. I mean, I would find living in a suburban situation where I had a congregation of blond, blue-eyed people, who had Morris Minor shooting brakes, cottages in Wales, and voted Liberal – all estimable things that we all aim for! – I would find that monochrome. Brixton is exciting! It is the way of the future, the Britain of the twenty-first century, in the sense of Britain being more cosmopolitan then, of people being more interested in a lot more issues, to do with society and its values.

'The *world* comes here – we live in a global village, going to school with Africans, West Indians, people speaking Turkish . . . There's going to be no turning back: our children will live in a sophisticated world where communications and travel are natural, and the narrower village world where one is entrapped in certain structures will have disappeared. It is very important for us to learn the skills we will need.'

Father Dennen is an American from Joy Street, Boston. Asked what brought him over here, he will say, 'The weather . . . I was misinformed.' He began to build experience of inner city problems in nearby Vauxhall where the community was also suffering the problems of post-war housing 'solutions', and experiencing evolutionary pangs of demographic change. 'I learned to say Mass at St. Peter's Vauxhall, a Pearson church. It's marvellous, even nicer than my church here because it's so gloomy. I *love* gloomy churches!'

In Vauxhall, he delved into the historical fabric of the area with the same irrepressible enthusiasm that he directed towards its social problems, and uncovered much of interest to gardening enthusiasts: 'Until recently the vicarage at St. Peter's was a house built by Tradescant to "manage" the old Vauxhall gardens which he himself designed. Tradescant was gardener to Charles II, but a sophisticated man, very rich and very clever – besides gardening he developed collections of painting, porcelain, and furniture. The roads in the parish follow the lines of the gardens, and you can still find mulberry trees planted by him. His influence can be seen everywhere. Have you ever wondered how the Oval got its shape? It was a mulberry tree plantation

135

for the silk factory that Charles II was going to build; if you look at the original design of Tradescant's gardens you will see the Oval in the exact place that it is today, and some of the seventeenth-century mulberry trees still survive.'

A Garden in the City

'The church at Kennington was founded by a man called Edward King, who later became Bishop of Lincoln, in what was darkest England in the mid-nineteenth century. King had this vision of the church as 'a garden in the city', a place of beauty that would bring beauty out of the local people. So our church was the first great Anglo Catholic church built in South London, and it is filled with beautiful things, carvings, vestments – so spectacular that the V & A have borrowed our vestments, chalices and so on, for exhibition. But the point is that all these beautiful things were made within the boundaries of the parish. The church is a monument to King's belief that the Gospel is beautiful and brings beauty out of others. And in many ways the theme of the garden is the same.'

The basic plan is a rosary, a central circle of free-form, old fashioned English roses, off which lead a series of different rooms and different perspectives. The visitor is encouraged to look down tunnels of plants, discover new parts of the structure – elements of the visionary experience, perhaps. It's

Apple trees bent into the shape of a tunnel leading towards a vignette of St. Francis.

St. John's was founded by Edward King, who had a vision of the church as a garden in the city.

overwhelming just like an inner city is overwhelming, yet the rooms themselves provide a sense of order, and their difference a sense of variety in the appreciation of the whole. 'It's meditative in that you go from space to space; it's visionary in that you look down places; and it's also chaotic in that I don't have time to do it!

'The plant plan is to create areas of intense "bangs" of colour that are timed; suddenly certain areas will come alive, like the roses now. This fits in with the theological ideas – we've got intense variety here; suddenly you look at one aspect (housing, jobs, school, race relations, Third World justice) or on one culture, or on one group of people growing and lively and exciting, and then next week you look in another direction and there'll be something else.

'It's a wonderful place for kids because you can hide behind things, and there are circles and little

Gateway to one of the rooms, formed by the arching branches of a cherry tree.

rooms and passages, and wonderful for garden fêtes and classic vicarage things.'

Beyond the garden and linked to it by a door in the garden wall is a new parish centre. 'It will have a large unit for old people, youth clubs . . . there'll be five social workers working there in an organisation called Welcare dealing with single Mums and children at risk, and so on. So can you imagine what part the garden will play? A lot of our single Mums are in Bed and Breakfast accomodation, so when they come to the centre, they can have lunch and use the garden.' Next to the centre, he is building alms houses to an eighteenth-century design, and there is an old vicarage to be used for young single homeless. 'Who pays for all this?' I ask naively. 'There's been no public money, it's all raised by us by begging bowl: private charities, church fêtes, trusts; the City has been generous.'

Philadelphus and climbing roses abound, everything intermingles. It's overwhelming just like an inner city is overwhelming, but the rooms provide a sense of order. It's a wonderful place for kids who run around and hide.

THE GARDEN AT
St. Winnow

The Reverend Canon and Mrs. H. Miles Brown

'There was something lovely about the old vicarage, the big house that stood in the middle of a community; it was really part of our heritage, and we have thrown it away.'

The Reverend Ernest Saunders

The vicarage and church of St. Winnow stand, and have done for centuries, on the east bank of the River Fowey which rises on Bodmin Moor and winds its way down through the Lostwithiel valley, and into the sea at the small but busy port whose name it bears. On a still, warm day in late spring, when the water is high, we wander along a lane which connects vicarage and church, and find absolute peace. Someone points out that parts of the film, Poldark, were photographed down here, and as we take in the timeless, quintessentially Cornish scene it does seem probable, though oddly disappointing.

'The vicarage was built before town and country planning,' says Mrs. Miles Brown. 'In those days you just chose your spot, and this was a pretty good one wasn't it!' 'It was built in the 1740s and enlarged about 1810,' continues her husband, a writer and local historian as well as leading churchman. 'Robert Walker, who was parson here at that time, purchased the Manor as well as farming his glebe. He was one of those "improving" Georgian parsons and he was here for fifty-three years as resident. He wasn't a

Ancient tombstones fashioned into the traditional Celtic cross.

Garden view of the church.

stemmed, golden double daffodil, very delicate blooms. They are followed by a mass of wild garlic, again very pretty but if you start to walk on it you'll never shake the smell.'

'I was once ill-advised enough to do my parish visiting after walking down here and noticed I wasn't quite as welcome as usual,' agrees the Canon as we pass by an old stone roller, once drawn by a donkey across the magnificent lawn, but now 'honorary retired' and too heavy to move. Symbol of another time, it recalled the Victorian practice described for us by Mrs. John Hole of Caunton Grange, of clothing these donkeys in little boots to protect the grass from their hoofs.

Little is known about the history of the garden at St. Winnow, though an old grotto furnished with slabs from the original kitchen was discovered by accident by son Jonathan when he fell into it. 'We also know that there was a conservatory at the

At the bottom of the garden the bright colours of rhododendron and azalea attract the eye towards the focal point of the garden's view – the church and river. Beyond, a mulberry and the silhouette of a Canadian maple.

gardener himself because of course in those days he had staff to do it for him; the vicarage was self-sufficient and very much the centre of employment in the parish: the girls in the kitchen, the boys on the farm and in the garden. Right up to the First World War the parson here enjoyed a staff of five. In fact the then gardener boy died only recently; he was over 80 and a garage proprietor in Truro.'

A wide sweep of well-kept grass rolls down from the house towards the ancient church, tucked in a fold of farmland between garden and estuary. 'In autumn the leaves turn, and when you look out in the morning, the lawn is covered with huge hand-like falls from the large Canadian maple – yellows, deep reddy browns, bronzes and russet colours.' Today, in May, the rhododendrons and azaleas, planted at the far end of the lawn to draw the eye towards the river, are in full bright flower. Mrs. Miles Brown and her husband have done everything to enhance this marvellous view, first by clearing it of encumbrances and then by leaving it well alone, a solution that a more obsessional plantsman might have found difficult to realise.

'On the south-west side of the lawn, beneath the maple and two splendid copper beeches, we have clumps of naturalised daffodils from the end of February, old-fashioned Lent lilies and the short-

The former stable yard, grassed over and planted with early crocus, runs down to a white gate leading into a wooded and semi-wild area of the garden.

south-west corner of the vicarage which came down on Father Capel in 1933,' the Canon continues, and in its place Mrs. Miles Brown has planted St. John's Wort, a spiraea 'Anthony Waterer', a climbing rose 'Golden Showers' and a cotoneaster to flank a path leading towards a door in an old brick wall. 'The cotoneaster produces lovely white flowers but never any berries. I don't know whether it's the birds that take them.' Birds are indeed a problem in a place as peaceful as this – there is nothing to scare them away, but Ernest Saunders, who is with us, has other thoughts and suggests that sulphate of potash at the base of the plant might do the trick.

We walk through the door under a rampant Russian vine which has grown up towards a huge, green water tank on the side of the vicarage – 'At times it covers the tank, you see we're all very rustic here, we're not on the mains,' explains Mrs. Miles Brown. The path leads into a 'secret' walled garden of colour where once stood a large wing for servants – 'a buttery, bakery, laundry, brewhouse and so on. When we came it was just brambles and old tins.' Here the Canon's wife indulges a passion for colour. Hydrangeas, honeysuckles, pink and cream spiraeas and an energetic elaeagnus, grown from a cutting that obviously enjoyed its cool moist position. In keeping with the Cornish soul of the place, there is a small sculptural vignette of the last independent Celtic bishop of Cornwall being reconciled with the Saxon Archbishop of Canterbury, made by the same

The agapanthus, an inspired departure from the usual blue.

artist as one which occupies a position above the west doors of Truro Cathedral. 'He came to me for details, and then gave me this copy by way of thanks,' the Canon explains.

On they lead us past traditional Victorian

The wild border. Celandine, primrose, campion, stitchwort, bugle, wood avens, lady's bedstraw and Jack-by-the-hedge. Candytuft and Lamiastrum variegatum in foreground.

Kenstec, the last independent Celtic Bishop being reconciled to the Saxon Archbishop of Canterbury.

variegated laurel plantings, a garden of ease built over the cobble stones of the old stables, which leads to a white gate flanked by golden privet and an ancient japonica. On the south side, reaching out from a huge flowering bay tree, is a mixed border – 'The Queen Elizabeth' roses underplanted with *Alchemilla mollis*, yellow flag irises, *Rudbeckia speciosa* 'Goldsturm', geums, Oriental poppies, agapanthus, Korean chrysanthemums, sidalcea, interspersed with azalea, *Camellia x williamsii* 'Donation', lilac, and *Ilex* 'Golden Gem'. Opposite, a natural border of wild plants jostle for a share of the sun's light and warmth. Round the north and back of the house, grass slopes newly cleared of overgrown laurel and saplings are home to junipers, cupressus, thuja, hawthorn, *Salix matsudana* 'Tortuosa' (twisted willow) and a handsome, fan-shaped *Rhus cotinus coggygria purpureus*.

This is a big garden, not one that can be looked after during an hour at the week-end. The 'great' dissolution of our rectories and vicarages was supposed to have been a solution for problems of maintenance and economy, and naturally enough talk, over tea, turns to the future of the vicarage here.

I remark that the house must surely soon come under the parsonage committee's hammer, but there has been no question of it so far. In theory Canon Miles Brown could stay until he dies because he had freehold tenure before measures were passed to ensure freehold reversion when an incumbent turned 70, though in fact the Canon will move if he retires. In the country at large, the economic arguments for dissolution have been seriously undermined as small new houses prove as costly and problematic as the old, and of course they are worth less to the Church as assets, on which other money might be raised. But what loss to the community at St. Winnow, I wonder, if eventually the house and garden is sold after his retirement? Does the Canon think that the vicar should live in the lap of his people? Is the idea of the vicar in the big house by the church old-fashioned, even offensive today?

He measures his answer carefully, 'Whether the parson is closer or more in tune with his people depends very much on what the parson *is*, not where he lives. Just because you've got six chimneys and your parishioners have only got two doesn't in itself make all that difference in outlook unless you already have a problem. Indeed you can very often share your frustrations and worries of a big house in understanding the frustrations and worries of an ordinary cottage. Really it turns on how you make use of the house, for instance here we have Tuesday Club meetings, Mothers Union meetings, Church Councils, *ad hoc* things of various kinds, the garden

The vicarage from beneath the huge Canadian maple; the dense carpet of wild garlic in the foreground.

fête and so on, because we have the room. When they waffle on, as they did at one parsonage committee recently, "Well we don't provide houses for use by the parish and their fêtes,"·and so on. That's plain ridiculous, as if every country parish had a commodious hall in its midst. That is cutting off your parson from the community.'

All arguments, economic or pastoral, seem to pall in the face of the house itself and the view through the long drawing room windows down to the river. Mrs. Miles Brown gets to the point: 'This house, you warm to it, like you do to so many of our old vicarages and rectories. We did immediately, even when we first came in and it was so dilapidated and down-at-heel . . . Our elder daughter was 4 when she was brought here for the first time and it was explained to her that we might be coming to live here. I remember she leant against the archway and I heard her say, "Dear old house, not had anybody to love you, *we'll* come and love you!" The child sensed something and I've always felt it. This house has a warmth and above all a feeling of continuity with the people that have gone before. It is so important to feel some sort of identity and belonging with your forebears.'

The church at St. Winnow.

Inkpen

Sir Fred and Lady Warner

'The important thing in a great French garden is not the garden but the fact that as a setting it enhances the importance of the people who walk and converse in it. It has no interesting detail; the visitors or the owners provide that, in their own persons.'

Edward Hyams

'The parish of Inkpen, or more correctly Ingpen lies at the extreme south-west corner of the county of Berkshire on the borders of Wiltshire and about 4 miles south-east by south of Hungerford, at the foot of the Downs which form the natural boundary between the counties of Berkshire and Hampshire.' So begins the history of the parish written in 1945 by its then rector, Francis J. Driscoll. There is some confusion as to the origins of its extraordinary name, Driscoll claims that its first syllable was derived from "Inga", the name of a Saxon chieftain, and that "pen" means an enclosure or stockade – Inga's stockade, whereas an article published in *Country Life* two years earlier claims that each of the two syllables means 'hill'.

But the real confusion, perhaps even controversy, relates to the unique garden of Inkpen Rectory. Driscoll has no qualms in stating that the rectory was built by the Revd. Brickenden in 1695 and that its garden was 'designed by the great landscape gardener, Le Nôtre, who designed and laid out so many gardens for Louis XIV, including the gardens at Versailles.'

Of Brickenden, little is known except what was written by Hearne during the run-up to the 1710 election of a new Master for Pembroke College in Oxford. The election was between Brickenden and another, named Hunt. '[Both candidates] have the Reputation of being Honest Men (that is, Tories), and endued with true Church of England Principles, but then there is this difference between them: Mr. Brickenden has seven Children, Mr. Hunt not above two or three; Mr. B. is an illiterate Person, Mr.H. a man of learning; Mr. B. is a boon Companion, or, as some style it, a Sot, Mr. H. is a man of Sobriety and discretion and came recommended by the Letters of the Bp of Bathe and Wells.' Hearne seems to have had

some justification for his appraisal since although the Rector of Inkpen was duly elected Master, four years later he died of apoplexy.

Andre Le Nôtre's gardens represent the apogee of classical garden design. The most outstanding can still be seen at Versailles, Vaux-le-Vicomte, Saint-Cloud and Chantilly. But besides the well-known examples of his work, he designed hundreds of other gardens, many for private owners throughout France, and also some in Germany, Italy, Belgium and England. At his death in 1700, the Duc de Saint-Simon wrote, 'He worked for private people as for the King with the same application – seeking only to aid nature and to attain the beautiful by the shortest road.'

Among the gardens with which he has been credited in England are St. James's Park, Greenwich Park and the semi-circular garden at Hampton Court as well as Kensington Gardens and Chatsworth. Although there is no certain documentation, it is at least conceivable that Inkpen was also his inspiration.

However, Sir Fred Warner, the owner of Inkpen Rectory since 1984, departs from Driscoll and the opinion of other previous owners of the rectory, by seriously doubting that Le Nôtre designed the garden or even that the rectory was built before Le Nôtre's death. 'When we came here we were told that the house was built in 1693 and that the gardens had been laid out at the same time. However, recently, we have received a good deal of information from Pembroke College in Oxford where Brickenden was Master, and it would appear that he only occupied this living from 1705 onwards. It seems very unlikely that he would have built the house so long before he got here. After being here for three years the whole idea appears to me to be ludicrous and unsupported

The illustration shows the original layout of the garden at Inkpen.

As Le Blond asserted, parterres are governed by the disposition of the land on which they are constructed, and at Inkpen this has meant an assymetrical design with four vistas culminating at the south-west corner. The vista walls are composed of beech, holly and the original yew; a number of large trees have been removed from the enclosures and new more suitable plantings are being made by Sir Fred Warner. Unfortunately, there is no evidence of what had been planted in these enclosures originally.

The kitchen garden is now a field where sheep graze, and its original purpose has been fulfilled by an old walled garden just north of the barn.

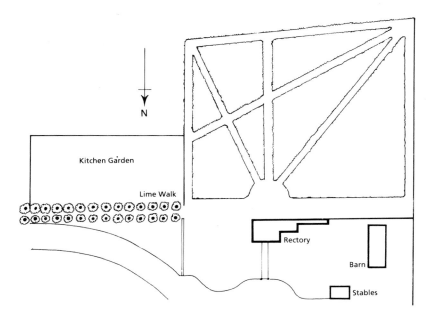

The lime walk looking down towards the main gate.

by any of the evidence. Did he ever *come* to England? I have consulted two or three garden historians on this, and there is no evidence that he did come. Secondly I cannot believe that if he had come here he would have spent time designing a garden for an obscure country clergyman in a tiny out-of-the-way part of Britain.'

Sir Fred is of the opinion that the garden was probably inspired by John James's translation into English of *The Theory and Practice of Gardening* by Le Sieur Alexander Le Blond, which contains illustrated plans of various parterres.

Alas, there is little in the Inkpen parterre itself to prove it one way or another. 'All Parterres are near alike,' wrote Le Blond, 'the Subject being exhausted in five or six Designs, one always falls into the same Track, and the Form becomes almost common; but

general Dispositions are always different, 'tis the Situation of the Place that governs them . . .'.

But while publication of John James' translation did, doubtless, inspire many copies of Le Nôtre's work in this country, the book did not in fact appear in England until 1728, long after the garden at Inkpen was laid out, by anyone's estimation.

Furthermore, claims that Le Nôtre never came to England at all, are not justified by history, for we know that shortly after Charles II came to the throne he asked Louis XIV of France whether he would permit Le Nôtre to work for him, and the French king's reply is recorded thus: 'Although I always have need of Le Nôtre, who is very occupied with work for me at Fontainbleau, I shall willingly permit him to make the trip to England since the King desires it.' There is also a warrant dated October 25th, 1662, permitting 'Le Nôtre, the King's architect to transport six horses to France custom free as by Royal warrant recited of the twenty-first of the same.'

The dispute may never be settled satisfactorily, and Inkpen does indeed seem rather out-of-the-way to justify the master's personal attentions. What seems most likely is that the design was commissioned by Brickenden from one of Le Nôtre's superintendents. According to Helen Fox's biography, when Le Nôtre first came to England he was too busy to do more than carry out the king's design commissions, and left his work to be supervised by assistants, and doubtless it was largely through these assistants that the art of classical design spread in England. We know, too, that Le Nôtre was quite happy for people to use his name, for when he was approached by the Duke of Portland to design the

The 'high spot' where 4 vistas converge. 'Originally the walls would all have been yew but in the 1840s everything began to deteriorate and holes were filled up with beech and holly to give lightness and variety,' says Sir Fred.

An arrangement of old yews on a mound at the east corner, the highest point of the parterre from which one could obtain a 'bird's-eye-view' of the whole effect.

Royal gardens at Kensington, he happily despatched his nephew, Claude Desgots, in his place, pleading infirmity and old age.

The garden at Inkpen, laid out as illustrated here, is now the subject of intensive (and expensive) restoration by Sir Fred and his wife Simone, a monumental task in which they are aided by their full-time gardener, Nigel. As Le Blond asserted, parterres are governed by the disposition of the land on which they are constructed, and at Inkpen this has meant an assymetrical design and an artistic 'high spot' (traditionally a sudden panorama of the outer world – here, a marvellous view of Inkpen Beacon) at the south-west corner of the two-acre site, where four vistas converge.

The lime walk – originally the trees' branches met in a leafy arch overhead – is also under repair. The Warners have rooted out all the bastard plants from the hedge that connects one lime to the next (sycamore, field maple and so on), and pollarded the overgrown trees to recover their original formal appearance. In three years the progress is, to say the least, impressive. But the *pièce de resistance*, in 1987, is without doubt Simone's inspired 'theatre' on the West side of the house. Out of what once was a sloping lawn she has created a spacious auditorium,

'a croquet lawn during the day and a theatre for musical frolics at night'. It looks up to a terrace planted with young beeches that will soon form a hedge, and three arches through which the performers will enter. 'One day we will consider doing a summer festival to raise money for charity, the old barn is big enough to house a musical or theatre group,' says Simone. Nearly 300 years after its inception, it seems that Inkpen is again coming to life, and this time we *know* who is responsible.

Nuneham Courtenay

Dr. Eileen Richardson

'I have a reverence for the place, its history . . . and in planting things – especially trees one can become a part of that.'

The rectory at Nuneham Courtenay, situated on what was once the Estate of Lord Harcourt and which now belongs to Oxford University, began life just over 200 years ago in a spirit of some turbulence. According to Walpole, Lord Harcourt, a founder member of the Dilettanti Society, was 'a marvel of pomposity and propriety', one of a band of cultural elite whose travels to Italy were to inspire the reproduction in England of the classical landscape style of gardening. This 'new' style of gardening required great space, some vigorous land moulding (valleys, lakes, and so on), the planting of woods and monuments (temples, ruins, etc.), all apposite to the classical theme and a picturesque view of Nature. In 1761, the village of Nuneham Courtenay became the subject of one such experiment, and was designed by Capability Brown.

Harcourt's initial problem was that the village literally stood in his way. As Mavis Batey explains in her pamphlet, 'Nuneham Courtenay: An Oxfordshire 18th-Century Deserted Village': 'Old Newnham Courtenay had been situated in a delightful position on a spur of the Chilterns which thrust out over the Thames plain; but, unfortunately, the features that its early settlers had chosen with a view to survival, the rising ground, the bend in the river and the fertile valley, were also most desirable for landscaping.' So it was, that Lord Harcourt determined to move the whole village – which included farms, a corn mill, ale-houses, and school – a mile or so down the road. A row of new homes was built either side of the turnpike (today, the chaotically busy Henley to Oxford road), each house exactly the same in appearance as the next – a sort of 18th-century council estate, and its name was changed from Newnham to Nuneham Courtenay.

The Poet Laureate, William Whitehead, wrote that the whole procedure was effected 'without a sigh', but as he had accompanied Lord Harcourt on his Grand Tour of Italy and remained a close friend, perhaps we should not rely on his opinion as fact.

One has to admire Harcourt's style, however, for when one villager stubbornly refused to budge – Babs Wyatt by name (she wanted to remain where her Colin 'breathed his last'), the Earl relented and turned the problem to his advantage by making Babs's 'clay-built cot' into a special attraction (real rusticity) for his fashionable guests.

The mediaeval church in the village posed slightly more of an obstacle in that it was consecrated ground and required Episcopal permission to remove. But eventually convinced of the Lord's good intentions, the Bishop of Oxford agreed to Harcourt's request to knock it down and build instead an ornamental church on rising ground some distance away. The resultant Greek Temple became the major focal point of his garden – 'the principal feature in one of the most beautiful landscapes in the world' – but also seemed to symbolise the artificiality of the whole enterprise in that its domed roof and pillared

The new church, focal point of Capability Brown's design.

A page from Newton's Diary, April 5th, 1761 – Old Lady Day – on which, appropriately, Newton prayed by Dame Well's mother and sent her some plum pudding and rabbit. Other than that, on 5th, 6th and 7th, work on garden and glebe continues, Bullock acting temperamental about his wages and treatment by Newton, and the poor puppy being 'fastened' to the house.

elegance gave way to a whitewashed austerity within iron-grilled, glass doors.

It must have made an odd sight, the Nuneham peasants trooping up the hill to Sunday service in a Greek Temple! Indeed, falling attendance figures would seem to indicate that the local populace did not entirely share their Lord's enthusiasm for 'Greek taste and Roman spirit'.

A rectory and newly consolidated glebe lands also formed part of Lord Harcourt's plan. It made a good deal of sense in those days to have the rector on your side. And the Revd. James Newton, duly rewarded with enhanced tithes, more profitable glebe lands and a greatly improved style of living, waived any objections he may have felt about the whole project, apparently entering into the 'spirit of change' even to the point of purloining the odd tombstone from the churchyard for his new garden.

'September 2nd. Went with bricklayer to the churchyard for an old gravestone to lay by pump and with much difficulty got it here.'

And if sometimes the whole business got him down, he was not averse to supplementing his diet by pinching some of Lord Harcourt's harvest for himself (his own new kitchen garden being yet virgin soil):

'April 7. Ate part of a cold Rabbit for Dn. Self got Greens and Radishes from my Lord's Garden.'

Newton took very seriously the task of moving his plants from old garden to new, his interest in horticulture stemming from his father whose *Complete Herbal* he had published in 1752. In this, as in the management of his glebe lands he co-opted the assistance of a man called Bullock, a rather confusing choice in the context of such diary entries as 'Bullock draw'd Mole towards the Flower Garden'.

We learn that an orchard of forty trees was planted, 150 other trees were bought for garden and glebe, bushes were moved from 'the Hanging Lands' (part of the glebe) to the rectory, hurdles were drawn and vineyards planted, and Bullock busied himself riding to and fro between Nuneham and Oxford buying plants and selling barley to pay for them. Soon after the work began, and much to Newton's annoyance, Bullock demanded increased wages to match the sudden increase in his reponsibilities. All round, it seems to have been a case of money in the right pocket winning the day.

Today the rectory is the property of Dr. Eileen Richardson and her husband, a barrister at the Old Bailey, having been sold by the Church in 1969. Part of the original house still stands, though a rector subsequent to Newton and obsessed by the drafts and damp of the old house, re-built one half of the L-shaped building in 1820. However, Newton's 'bow-room' with marble chimney-piece and 'great ceiling picture' mentioned in his diary, still commands a marvellous view of the wood he planted with its huge Cedar of Lebanon, tulip tree, hollies, sycamores and Spanish chestnuts making their stately way down a sculpted valley, which falls steeply from the south-west aspect of the house to a stream and distant view of the Thames near Oxford. Newton's 'crinkle-crankle' walled garden – for him a vegetable and fruit garden, its wavy walls providing

Distant view of the Thames from the lawn above the wood.

welcome protective nooks for nectarines, peaches, and other cordoned fruit – also survives today, and the Richardsons have grassed it, planted a vista of apple trees beside a swimming pool and barbecue, thrown up a 'Nevada', an 'Iceberg', a montana over its ancient walls, and are now embarking upon an ambitious plan to revitalise old Newton's vegetable beds.

Along the outside face of the south wall Dr. Richardson has planted an herbaceous border –

The wall Newton built to provide protection for his nectarines, peaches and other fruit.

birthday present to her husband – made of old bush roses, delphiniums, pinks, broom, lavender, weigela, phlox, paeonies, geranium (cranesbill), wild campion and lots of blue and white campanula.

But overall, 'restoration' is the key word, something that a rector today could never hope to achieve on such a scale.

Seven years ago, Dr. Richardson heard that the property was for sale, but came to look with barely serious intentions – indeed, on that day, the house appeared so intimidating that she would have circled the driveway and driven off had its owner (the first lay owner of Nuneham Rectory) not burst from the house and insisted she at least look round. The 1820 re-build had added to its elegance and she fell in love with what she saw, in her excitement barely noticing let alone exploring its garden.

'We had had about an acre of garden in Hertfordshire,' she recalls. 'Flowers, herbaceous borders and shrubs were the size of my concept of a garden. It has taken me five years to come to terms with the scale of this. The reality of what we had taken on began to dawn when, barely a week after we arrived, one huge branch of the cedar came down in a storm . . .'

Dr. Richardson called up a forestry man who came and chopped up the branch and tended the cedar's wound. While he was there they began to investigate the rest of the wood together, discovering other fallen trees, impenetrable undergrowth, brambles and massive laurel and rhododendron bushes, all hallmarks of a rectory garden sadly let go. In that first year it cost £3,000 clearing and making the wood passable, other than on hands and knees. Today, the wood is Dr. Richardson's main pleasure in the garden – 'In Spring, we become obsessed with it!'

Like all the oldest preserved rectory gardens there is a 'secret' walk – 'I am anxious to keep this part as a garden of enclosures, a romantic garden with secrets.' We make our way down a narrow path, barely 2 feet wide, hemmed in by laurel bushes tipped with bright-green new growth. It has just been raining and the fresh Spring-green air at the edge of the wood begins noticeably to increase in humidity as we descend a densely planted, sloping path – 'Watch out!' Dr. Richardson exclaims. 'We have two deer living down here; they make the path even more slippery than it might be.' Suddenly we are released from the constraints of laurel into a misty clearing

Above: 'The reality of what we had taken on began to dawn when, barely a week after we arrived, one huge branch of the cedar came down in a storm.' Right, the clearing in the woodland walk, planted with willows, prunus, whitebeam, wild cherry and acer.

The southern corner of the rectory glimpsed through the arms of a cedar tree.

The path leading to the azaleas and a flowering cherry.

planted with weeping willows, prunus, whitebeam, wild cherry, and acer – foils, in February, for a sea of aconites, and at any time silent vanguards for a majestic line of shimmering poplars that rise some 60 feet above. 'I'm worried about these being so tall,' she says, 'I believe their time span is quite short . . .'

Moving on, we climb upwards past a mass of philadelphus, and catch a glimpse of the southern corner of the rectory through the arms of the enormous cedar. Now down the slope again, by another path, we hear the ripple of water from the stream on the valley floor. Here another of Dr. Richardson's projects is in progress. What is now home for marsh marigolds, brought from her native Ireland, is soon to become a haven for bog and shade-loving hostas and ferns, irises and astilbes. Just above the line of the stream, we come to a closed-in, colourful plateau of azaleas and a little, recently planted flowering cherry. On this steamy, rain-soaked day, the closeness of atmosphere emphasises the womb-like security created beneath the canopy of trees – it makes an environment in which she feels able to relax completely and it is her favourite place to sit. 'I like being solitary in a garden, being able to walk round on my own in the morning without anyone feeling I am at all eccentric. I just wander and think how wonderful it all is. I have a reverence for the place, its history . . . and in planting things – especially trees, one can become a part of that.'

THE GARDEN AT
Pelynt

Mr. James Parkes

**'The secret inner places of the garden
my mother was never acquainted with, naturally.
They were children's property . . .'**
Geoffrey Grigson

Any visitor to the old vicarage garden at Pelynt in Cornwall, arriving at dusk on a late spring evening will be met by a strange echoing sound of bird calls, quite inaudible from the road outside. The reason for this eerie surprise is that the garden drops down steeply below the level of the road into a valley, and forms an echo chamber beneath a canopy of giant elms, California redwood, chestnuts, beeches and sycamores – stalls for Nature's choir of rooks, owls and other noisy night-life. The cawing and hooting is amplified by the leafy procenium, and given a 'glassy', almost transparent effect by a cold, wet, 'sounding board' of a stream, which scores the valley bottom behind a grassy, terraced 'stage'.

'Pelynt is in east Cornwall, not far from the sea, some 20 miles within the county, 4 miles from Looe, 3 miles from Polperro, 5 miles from Fowey, in a block of land bounded by the deep valley of the Looe River, on the west by the wider "ria" or sunken valley of the Fowey. It is an old parish devised mainly out of the two ancient manors of Pelynt and Trelawne.' So begins the story of the parish (*Freedom of the Parish*) written by the late son of one of its vicars, the well-known writer and poet, Geoffrey Grigson. Grigson was born at Pelynt Vicarage in 1905, the youngest of seven brothers when his father – not a Cornishman – was 'a month short of sixty'.

It seems that Mrs. Grigson never came to terms with the strange effect cast upon the vicarage garden by its trees, which became for her a symbol of all she disliked about the place: 'My mother . . . who felt Cornwall (she should have crossed out Cornwall and put her life) as a prison, felt also that the trees, which no doubt were too numerous, shut her in and round and overhead . . . She had a campaign of hatred for years against two or three elms across the stream, without ever getting my father to act against them.

The house from beneath the dense canopy of trees. Geoffrey Grigson's mother never came to terms with the gloom.

Certainly a damp, heavy green gloom hung under all the thick trees by the height of the summer.'

The house was built in 1841 for a vicar named Kitson, whose daughter (known as 'Black Harriet' by villagers, 'who were short and quick with her faults', and by Grigson as 'a satin-clad dragoness') rose to become the second wife of the village baronet, Lord Trelawney.

Among the shadowy predecessors of Vicar Kitson was one Joshua Howell who held Pelynt for sixty years from 1725, kept its cellars replete with fine wines, was responsible for planting the garden's huge sycamores, and complained of the 'sad and tumbled state' of the original house with its 'earthen floors'.

By the time Vicar Grigson arrived on the scene, however, the 'new' vicarage was in sad repair: 'I

Inside the closed-in leafy walk on the far side of the stream.

Where brother Lionel made 'shrewd, far-controlled water-wheels on the fall of the stream.'

belt of laurels and sycamores; jabbing on the way at a plantain or two, or a dandelion.'

. . . of his brother Kenneth who 'wheeled me at speed in a wheelbarrow up and down the paths of the garden, making station and halts, Rubbish Heap Station, Umbrella Tree Station, Bridge Station, Lavatory Station, All Change! – it was a rare, powerful, unforgettable proceeding which I remember with the deepest satisfaction.'

. . . of the chestnuts and gigantic laurels through which 'came the noises of a community, the sawyers in their pit on one side of the Green . . . the ringing of iron on iron from the two smithies, the passing of carts and waggons.'

. . . of his brother Lionel making 'shrewd, far-controlled water-wheels on the fall of the stream . . .'

In *The Crest on the Silver*, Grigson's is a marvellous account of a Victorian vicarage in its twilight years and evocation of the wonder and joy that the rambling house and garden provided the imagination of one small boy. 'The garden which spread away from the house had been the masterpiece of Colonel Cox's planning. He had cut terraces from the main terrace (in front of the dining-room and drawing-room windows and the sham window, half-hidden by a mixture of ivy and "Gloire-de-Dijon" and cotoneaster) down to the lawn; beyond which flowed a number of lazy and large rho-

grew up really into the period of decay,' his son recalls, 'when the holes in the lino were beginning to show the hall boards, when the old original wallpaper was beginning to stain and peel; and when the tea and coffee sets were seriously gapped by casualties. The garden grew less tidy. There were more weeds in the drive, and the hens (free of any run they may have had) began to scratch dusting holes among the roots of laurel and rhododendron. But the pattern was only scratched, not destroyed.'

The house and especially the garden provided a rich store of memories which lived with Geoffrey Grigson throughout his life – childhood memories

. . . of his father who 'went into his study after breakfast, smoked and thought, filled in some diocesan returns, or drew up some tithe notices; filled his pipe again, walked out into the hall and with his hat and a Dutch hoe went off down into a dell hung with hart's-tongue ferns to the romantic lavatory, which was built athwart the stream behind a safety

The 'dell hung with hart's tongue ferns' and 'the romantic lavatory, which was built athwart the stream behind a safety belt of laurels and sycamores'.

dodendrons hiding the stream. The main terrace ended in a long low wall over which one looked to the west, over fields and past elms to the heights of Goss Moor, fantastically cut into white mountains of the moon, sharp triangles of quartz from the china-clay pits. This wall started to rise in the corner, which was pierced by a round-arched, priestly doorway, leading down to the kitchen garden. On the terrace there were tea-roses, there was St. John's Wort, and inevitably, rising from it, a tall laurestinus. Dahlias, red and yellow, with long spurs, came up every year beside the dry stems of the previous year's growth; the frosts never being strong enough here in the west to damage the tubers, which no one thought of lifting. In the corner by the priestly door, there were tall old-fashioned fuchsias with flakey cinnamon stems; and the tall naked stem of a rose which climbed up the wall into the thick ivy along the top of it. The corner and the ivy made a darkness for the fuchsia stems and flowers to decorate.

'Down the drive were on one side the weeping ash, under which on a slope to the lawn and the stream grew crocuses and snow-drops; and then a clump of pampas grass, in which hedge-sparrows nested year after year. On the other side, first a

box-edged length of flowers and weeds, then a vast noble monkey-puzzle, the cones of which burst to shower nuts on the drive (the dead branches were useful as scimitars), and a hybrid horse-chestnut, the pink and white flowers of which were of singular loveliness. There was another section of the garden across the stream, on the far side of the valley. At one end there was an orchard with some good trees, in

Clipped yew trees guide the eye down three terraced levels to the lower lawn (the 'stage') and woodland beyond.

Clematis montana on the wall leading to the large kitchen garden.

particular a quarrenden, giving apples red to the pips, a tree of small sweet summer apples, which must I think have been a yellow Ingestre, and a Cornish Aromatic and a Cornish Gillyflower; higher up, and in full view from the windows, the slope was commanded by the Big Fir Tree, a vast, dark stone-pine in an ivied fork of which the owls nested, and from which the hen bird could be flushed by a well-thrown stick into blunt flight through the trees. Daffodils shone from that slope over the rho-dodendrons to the drawing-room and the dining-room; and if one climbed either of the two easy beech trees above the Big Fir Tree, or the Big Fir Tree itself, the blue sea was visible three miles off beyond Polperro. Still of all things in this rich wild garden which I now love to remember, of all the oaks, the redwoods, and copper beeches and flowering shrubs planted by the ingenious Colonel Cox, of all the

pines, and the sycamores planted by a pluralist vicar in the eighteenth century, none count so much as the laurels. Their stems were long, clean, thick and black, in their strongest black after rain. Their leaves shone on spring mornings, as one leant from the bedroom windows. Their flowers, standing up precise and white from the glistening leaves, were one of the first natural excellences of which I was conscious, and I like them in spite of my mother's frequently uttered execration of their smell. I explored the strange depths of these laurels on a swing, from one of the chestnut trees, by which one could crash into their finer branches. They have helped to make that translation of Housman's

We'll to the woods no more
The laurels all are cut

a poem which is one of my private and intimate properties.

'This garden with its varying levels, its free-stone walls and its waterfall, provided the symbolic minia-tures, the first editions of every possible adventure and ambition. It seemed boundless to me at one time, with, always, some new shrubbery to be explored, some new thing to be found, some new tree to be climbed. Digging for worms once, I turned up a glass medallion, with name and date, from a wine-bottle of an eighteenth-century vicar. And there were rhododendron clumps under which grew those besoms of elm twiggery, coming out in the spring with leaves (see D. H. Lawrence) like a flutter of green snow.'

THE GARDEN AT

Falstone

The Reverend and Mrs J. A. Woodhead-Keith-Dixon

'Discovery and restoration is the theme. I'd known of the house long ago, but there hasn't been a garden here since before the last war. The idea is to open it all up again, let people see it coming back. They are all fascinated and delighted to see it coming back because in the country the church is still very much the centre of the community.'

The North Tyne valley, a mile or so from Falstone Rectory.

This is the North Tyne Valley – 'We're 500 yards from the North Tyne which wends its way into the South Tyne at Hexham and then on as the Tyne, to Newcastle.' Perched precariously on the side of a hill, the garden at Falstone commands sensational views but enjoys a very short flowering season – 'nine months winter and three months summer – July to September, and not two consecutive days of sun this year. There's no prevailing wind; it comes from every direction all at once!'

The Rector, Jamie, is conscious of history – characters from centuries of his own family's are subjects of oil paintings hanging from the walls of his most gracious Georgian home. Now he and his wife are determined to bring Falstone Rectory back to its one-time greatness, and make it once more a centre of parish life.

'Originally Falstone was taken out of the great

Falstone Rectory, isolated and subject to appalling weather conditions.

The terrace in front of the rectory looks down upon a field, all part of the Church property, and thence across more beautiful Northumberland countryside. The rector has made the most of the stunning views by clearing the terrace of all encumbrances and planting a colourful, low-lying bed of cultivated heathers, seathrift and dwarf French marigolds. Nearer the house the garden visitor picks his way through colourful ground-cover plants set between giant slabs of newly laid local-stone paving.

Polygonum bistorta 'Superbum', another element in the front terrace border.

The pool, under construction in 1986 after the sloping ground had been terraced, and in 1987 with various Hybrid Teas in attendance. The pathwork is all disused local stone brought painstakingly into position.

parish of Sandiburn, along with four other parishes in the area. Falstone alone occupies about 250 square miles, and in the eighteenth century the Rector of Sandiburn would travel the considerably wider area on horseback, holding a service once a month at our parish church. At that time the Earl of Derwentwater owned the land – he who was executed for his part in the 1715 uprising. All his land was commandeered by George I, but instead of giving it (as he was wont to do) to one of his mistresses, he gave it to the Greenwich Hospital with the proviso that they and the Admiralty should appoint a number of chaplains to serve the people in this wide area. But nothing was done for almost a hundred years, until after the battle of Trafalgar. When all the naval chaplains were coming out, they decided they'd better house them somewhere, so they built these homes for them. It happened at the end of the Georgian period, before they started building the Victorian monstrosities – so it was just at the right time!

'People used to travel miles and miles to come to all kinds of occasions here, and we want that to happen again. But when we arrived in 1982 the garden was beyond belief – dark, dismal and totally neglected . . . But because I knew the house of old, we felt it had possibilities.' However, site clearance involved more work even than surface conditions suggested: 'We removed ninety-six buckets of broken glass and pottery when digging out the pond.'

His first step was to open up the site to its splendid views. Darkening sycamores were felled, and a copper beach so close to the house that its branches dripped rainwater down the chimneys. Jamie then invited people from the parish to recall what the garden used to look like. 'The churchwardens might suggest that I try digging here or there, and perhaps I'd find a cobbled path; gradually the structure began to emerge.' He co-opted the help of a young man from the village and together they brought up local stone from the forest and from old forgotten walls. These became the retaining walls for new terraces and a 9-by-15-foot pool on what had been a field sloping down to the river.

Behind the house, Jamie's wife Clodagh has spent four winters clearing the woodland of brambles and holly to make a leafy walk. As her work progressed they were rewarded by the re-appearance of wild primroses, snowdrops, violets and bluebells, as these and the secondary plantings of rhododendrons responded to the newly lit conditions.

Falstone Rectory is a labour of love for them both, and goodness knows it would have to be in so difficult an environment as this. Following our first visit in 1986 we arrived in August a year later to take 'progress' photographs. Fortunately it was one of Falstone's few sunny days, but Clodagh was still bemoaning the loss of a vegetable garden, destroyed by constant rain – 'We only got a couple of pounds of peas out of four rows, practically no potatoes which had just rotted in the drenched soil – a few strawberries and a few carrots, some gooseberries and that was it.'

As if wind, rain and 'Northumberland midges' were not enough (on warm damp days the latter literally drive the gardener from his plot), moles had been an added curse. I tell him of the Revd. Symons, a champion leek grower from Mickley, near Stocksfield, who having unsuccessfully tried to make his leek beds mole proof, recently resorted to a shotgun to get rid of them. 'Trap them; smoke them,' threatens the Rector, 'but you've got to know how to lay the trap, where all the mole runs are and where the pests can get to. It's a complicated business.

Clematis tangutica cascades over an archway between pool and front garden.

They'll even come up in the middle of the tarmac!' 'They are incredibly strong,' agrees Clodagh. 'I caught one the other day. I actually saw one digging away and hastily brought a trowel and, catching sight of the back end of it, I grabbed it by one leg and pulled and pulled, but had "the *dickens* of a job" getting it out . . .'

Behind the house, the rector's wife has cleared the wood of decades of brambles and holly, revitalising secondary plantings of rhododendron, and wild primroses, snowdrops, violets and bluebells – perfect companions on a spring-time walk.

THE OLD PALACE GARDEN AT
Ely

Mr. and Mrs. John Russi

'"We're looking for a kind volunteer to bring the garden
back," someone said. "Right," I said, "we'll do it." We
were rather taken aback by the effusive thanks – what a lot
of fuss about one tree and a lawn. . .'

Mrs. Jean Walker, wife of the Bishop, greeted the suggestion of a visit to Ely with warmth and
enthusiasm, directing us to no fewer than six other gardens in her husband's diocese. She is herself
gardener-in-chief at The Bishop's House, a garden constructed over the site of the original
monastic living quarters and bounded on one side by the Cathedral's south wall. Its main features
include an enormous kitchen garden, a long herbaceous bed – a kaleidoscope of colour in summer,
and a formal rose garden looked down upon by England's second oldest wistaria. Beautiful
certainly, but right from the start Mrs. Walker felt there was a more important story to tell, a story

159

'little short of a miracle', which focuses on the restoration of another garden, just across the road.

The Old Palace at Ely was built in 1540 and from the mid-seventeenth century housed the bishops of what was then a most important diocese in the Church of England. The garden is famous not least because it contains the oldest plane tree in the country, named the Gunning plane after Bishop Gunning, who introduced it during the period of his episcopacy – 1675 to 1684. Nearly 300 years later two farmer gardeners, John and Diana Russi, found themselves in charge of more than 2 acres of great gardening history. Mrs. Russi explains how it came about:

'We became involved with the garden quite by accident. I had mentioned in passing that I was prepared to help the Sue Ryder Foundation, who were about to take over the Old Palace as a hospice, thinking that I could work with the patients in the home. Then one day the telephone rang and out of the blue a voice asked, 'Would you be prepared to help at a fund raising fête for the hospice?' When I said that I would, the voice continued that some help would also be required to clear the garden before the stalls could be set up.

'So it was that we went along, the day before the fête, and saw what looked to us to be really quite a small garden. There was a big plane tree and a lawn bounded by obviously ancient garden walls on two sides, the palace building on another and a split

Summer colour in Mrs. Walker's herbaceous border: dahlias, phlox, petunias, sedum, salpiglossis, sisyrinchium, begonias, white lilies, hollyhocks, lupins and delphiniums, and catching one's attention towards the Cathedral wall – sumach, robinia and eucalyptus trees.

chestnut fence rolled out across the fourth side in front of what looked like a tatty hedge.

'The next day we had the garden "do", and while it was going on someone said to me, "We're looking for a kind volunteer to bring this garden back; we can't find anyone." I immediately looked around and nudged my husband. I could tell he liked the idea too; it didn't seem so large. "Right," I said, "we'll do it." We were rather taken aback by the effusive thanks – what a lot of fuss about one tree and a lawn, we thought!

'The following day I thought I'd go along with paper and pencil and sketch one or two ideas of what we might do, and while I was there, still looking at this little lawn and big plane tree, I thought I'd just see how deep the hedge was the other side of the split chestnut fencing. Well, I climbed over and, my God! There was another acre of garden behind it! And, it was like a jungle! A 12-foot high jungle of rogue bamboo, rogue elder, rogue sycamore – you name it and it was there. I came back home to my husband and said, "Oh dear, it's a little bigger than we imagined."

'At this point we realised that we had no alternative but to break out our chain saws and bush cutters from storage. We had recently retired to Ely from the

The path to the pond at the Old Palace.

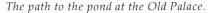

A section of the herbaceous border at the Old Palace, in its first season.

Swansea valley where we had been farmers, and had brought a lot of useful farming tools with us. So at least we had the right equipment to tackle the job.

Eventually we cut out so much stuff from the garden that three tractors and two of those big corn trailers were needed to cart it away. There was, literally, about 20 tons of rubbish. When you see the garden today, eighteen months later, it is hard to realise what it was like; you couldn't even see the pond, for example.

John Russi takes up the story, at the planning stage. 'A boy who had been confined to a wheelchair for six years probably influenced the planning more than anyone. Urging me to consider his plight in the design of the garden, he said: "If you'd been in a wheelchair for as long as I, you'd design a place so that wheelchairs can move about." Bearing this in mind we designed the path down to the pond so that the hospice wheelchair patients could feed the ducks.

'Indeed, that boy has made the whole garden an interesting experiment – no one who sees the rockery understands why we have terraced it like rice fields. But when we say, "Put yourself in a wheelchair," they understand completely that it's a garden for someone viewing from a child's height. Again, the paving into the greenhouse has been laid down so that the patients can use it, for this is where all the plants began – everything that we have put into the

'You can walk through the conifers, it's like a miniature maze.'

The pond, which is home for carp and ducks, is mentioned along with the Gunning Plane and gingko trees in a survey of the garden undertaken in 1865. Mr. and Mrs. Russi have also traced planting plans back to 1790 with the help of the Cambridge University library.

garden has been grown here from seed or cuttings.

'Across the lawn towards the pond, the original planting of conifers was clearly chosen for it's contrasting colours – you can walk through the trees, it's like a miniature maze. They were lost in the wilderness and dying from starvation when we arrived, but fortunately we caught them just in time. Reviving them took 6 inches of sheep manure and the hose turned on them constantly. Then, they exploded! If you use sheep manure, don't dig the mulch in, just leave it on top; it'll soon work its way down.

'On the other side of the conifer maze lies the newly seeded path down to the pond, which would have supported a heavy stick on its surface with all the green that lay on it before. Now that it's clean we have introduced seven golden carp and the ducks – they're ornamental so they won't fly away provided they're fed. There is one mallard, however; she might fly if it wasn't for the drakes to keep her quiet.

'Walking past the pond, we have the copper beech. In front of it were planted thirty-six lilies to see what would happen – they obviously like the damp, light shade so now I will reduce the shrub around them and they alone will provide colour to balance the brighter end of the garden. That's the idea at any rate and it seems to be working.

'As we go on you'll see that I've also tried some hydrangeas and they appear to like it too, so I shall supplement these to give a nice spot of colour as you walk around to the top end of the pond, where we will be planting shrub roses. They'll make marvellous cover and colour flowing down to the path. At the moment we have some temporary fill-ins, but as the shrub roses get bigger and bigger so I'll take them out to leave just the shrubs. We've got 'Albertine', 'Yvonne Rabier' and 'Compassion' climbing up the wall, and then we've got the usual ones: 'Penelope', 'Felicia', 'Cardinal de Richelieu', 'Ulrich Brunner' and 'Graham Thomas' – all the sort of lovely big, old-fashioned plants, with those old-fashioned scents and beautiful, beautiful shape. What we want to create is a sense of freedom, of wildness here.

'We shall have a bench under the copper beech for a good view of the pond. And then, in the foreground hard by the water, some irises are getting established. I've put out an SOS to the local Wicken Fen for the wild indigenous water lilies, and they've said they're going to give them to me when they do their thinning out in the autumn. The stonework in the middle of the pond was once a fountain, although there doesn't appear to be a point from which to feed

The ancient Cathedral at Ely, from the south side.

The Gunning Plane, the oldest plane tree in the world. Planted some time between 1675 and 1684 by Bishop Gunning of Ely, it was measured in 1983 and found to be 115 ft. high and 37 ft. in girth.

it. We know that it did work once, because one of the children who used to be here when the Palace was a handicapped school says that he remembers seeing it. But how it worked we just cannot fathom. It goes back at least as far as the 1860 survey.

'Here, as we walk round to the main lawn where we began, is the ginkgo and nearby is the Gunning plane. Planted by Bishop Gunning in the seventeenth century the plane tree was measured in 1983 as being 115 feet high and 37 feet in girth, and it's on the register of Historic Trees in England. Look at the tree surgery which they've recently done: when we got here we saw that the huge cables they'd put around the branches were cutting right in; in time of course they'd kill everything above them. So, as you can see, they put in a plate through which the whole tree is now laced together, and saved it for posterity. They also thinned the tree by a quarter as it was getting dangerously top-heavy. The man they had on the floor was obviously a tree artist; he re-designed the tree and the two men up top did the cutting, and kept the shape perfectly. In the process they had to make special bolts 4 feet long and special drills because 4-feet drills simply do not exist. Finally they had to work out how to take a 4-foot drill out of a tree when you're hanging on a rope!

Naunton

The Rt. Hon. and Mrs. Nicholas Ridley

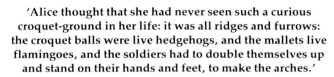

**'Alice thought that she had never seen such a curious
croquet-ground in her life: it was all ridges and furrows:
the croquet balls were live hedgehogs, and the mallets live
flamingoes, and the soldiers had to double themselves up
and stand on their hands and feet, to make the arches.'**

Lewis Carroll

Though it offers no clues – flamingo feathers or even
hoops – legend has it that the lawn in front of the Old
Rectory at Naunton was the inspiration for Lewis
Carroll's croquet green in *Alice's Adventures in
Wonderland*. Certainly, when the Reverend Litton
lived there in the 1860s, his close friend Canon
Charles Dodgson frequently came to stay, presum-
ably as relaxation from his duties as Lecturer in
Mathematics at Christ Church, Oxford, and all those

(somewhat less arduous) river trips down the Isis.
Today it is a bolt-hole of a different sort, the
week-end retreat and constituency home of the
Rt. Hon. Nicholas Ridley, M.P.

When we arrive, Mr. and Mrs. Ridley are already in
the garden, for gardening is their relaxation. Twenty-
nine years ago when Nicholas Ridley bought the
house he must have had more time for gardening
than the busy life of a Cabinet Minister allows, for

The wild Water Garden with over sixty varieties of primulas and some fifty-seven different willows.

what he has created is an imaginative 'mechanical' marvel of almost Heath Robinson proportions.

His source of inspiration and life of his plants is the River Windrush which ripples past the Old Rectory and, by dint of cleverly designed waterways, tunnels, aqueducts, islands, walls and bridges, is diverted into his garden to become the power source of his botanical creation, and then out again to continue its voyage through this lovely Cotswold village.

Such use of natural resources seems extraordinarily appropriate, and the resulting scene is idyllic, complete quietude orchestrated by the peaceful sounds of flowing water, plants colourful but not too bright, trees graceful but not tall and never dominant.

Mr. Ridley's design was originally conceived to provide a series of rooms providing distinctly different effects, the most impressive of which are a wild water garden nearest to the river source, and a formal

canal near the house. The wild garden plays host to primulas and willows – more than sixty varieties of the former, which provide colour (yellow through red to purple) from March to October, and some fifty-seven different varieties of willow, which give interest in winter with colourful bark (*Salix pendulifolia*) and in spring with catkins (the claret-coloured ones of *S.* 'Melanostachys'), as well as now, in summer, with their cool green leaves. Mr. Ridley understands that plants come much better (and less expensively) from seed, so practically everything in the garden has been cultivated from seed or cutting. The lesson is simple and difficult to fault: 'There is no need to spend a lot of money on a garden, we buy one of everything and then reproduce it.' As well as primulas there are campanulas, geraniums, dianthus, saxifrages, vincas, pulmonarias, and irises.

Nearby, another water garden is in progress, half formal, half informal, bounded by a low stone wall illustrated with signs of the zodiac. 'The Zodiac Garden will be a white garden,' says Mrs. Ridley, 'white primulas, of course, white irises, syringas,

The Canal Garden, flanked by sentry-style irises just coming into flower, the aqueduct is on the right.

A section of Mrs. Ridley's colourful border which makes a perfect foil for the straighter lines of her husband's design.

A weigela spills over the wall of the Canal Garden.

Looking towards the summer house, the design gives the illusion of it being much farther away than it is.

white potentillas and clematis, and white roses too.' One wonders what the paint-brush gardeners in *Alice* would do with that!

Adjacent, running from the main house at one end to a summer house (where much of the cultivation is done) at the other, is the formal canal, flanked sentry-style by irises, and swimming with trout. 'They're friends, really, we don't eat them.' A mature copper beech hedge grows down one side of the canal, planted when first they moved in. It leads (by means of a leafy archway) to criss-cross avenues not long planted with willows, and the resulting, uncut grassy enclosures with shrub roses, cherries, acers and crabs. There is also a nuttery with walnuts, almonds and sweet chestnuts.

Down the other side of the canal he has built an aqueduct to carry water to different parts of the garden. Standing at either end one is struck by the sheer work involved. Was it all mapped out first on paper? 'There was a plan for the part nearest to the house, but then it just *growed*,' he says. 'The idea is to

One of the avenues leading to the beech hedge, where once Alice's croquet green lay.

give an illusion of distance; the sides are not parallel, you see, they make the end seem farther away than it really is.' He designed and built all the structures in the garden, and I ask Mrs. Ridley whether there had been a training – 'He *was* trained as a civil engineer, but his sense of architecture is strong, probably because of his grandfather.' 'His grandfather?' I ask, knowing that I am probably being naive.

'Lutyens . . .'

Well, if Mr. Ridley has found an outlet for a talent inherited from the creator of New Delhi city centre, Ednaston Manor in Derby, and Gledstone Hall in Skipton, Yorkshire, he has also somehow managed to find, in Mrs. Ridley, a gardening partnership of a

nature not dissimilar to that which his grandfather enjoyed with Miss Jekyll. For in this garden Mrs. Ridley fulfils the role of colourist, looking after the informal plantings in the beds left by Mr. Ridley's designs. Here in the Canal Garden we see a herbaceous border of nepeta, roses, peonies, geraniums, sedums and *Lilium monadelphum*. 'This bed is all blues, pinks, and some yellow, and these colours go through the seasons. We have lilies and campanulas, paeonies then phlox, pinks, and then end up with sedums – all underplanted with small spring bulbs which are the first to show.'

Landscove

Mr. and Mrs. Raymond Hubbard

'A garden is one of three things; it may even be all of them:
a good-growing unit, a setting for leisure or play-piece, or
a work of art. No longer interested in the kitchen garden
aspect, my leisure is spent, for preference, in cities.'

Edward Hyams

The Oxford Movement so named because it began, in 1833, at Oxford, was a determined effort by orthodox theologians to rejuvenate the Church of England by means of sermons and writings. In Dartington, Devon, a certain Miss Louise Champernowe had got to know John Keble and John Henry Newman, two of the Movement's leading figures, and decided to do something practical to promote the Church in the area. Simultaneously her brother-in-law, vicar of nearby Staverton, fell ill and found the long Devon lanes and his widespread parish, which included Landscove, too much for him. The result was the division of his parish and a new church and vicarage which Miss Champernowe built high up on a hill overlooking Landscove.

The architect chosen was the then young John Loughborough Pearson, R.A., of Westminster, London, and the church was duly consecrated by Bishop Phillpotts of Exeter in 1851. One wonders whether 'the Phillpotts connection' (see *The Gardens at St. Feock*) influenced the choice of architect.

Church and vicarage together cost Miss Champernowe £3,000.   Both are remarkable buildings, miniature of course by comparison with Pearson's later work at Truro but almost bursting with the concentrated effect of their designer's ideas. Depending on viewpoint the vicarage could be taken for three or four quite different houses, yet it loses none of its homogeneity for that. In certain lights – its tall fir rookeries providing macabre choral accompaniment – it conjurs up Gothic visions that would have delighted Jane Austen's Catherine Morland, and Landscove's greatest gardener was to call one aspect 'Northanger Walk'.

Mr. Hubbard, its owner today, recalls his first visit to the place: 'It was a miserable, overcast and quite cold day in early April when we walked up the drive to the house. We had had to travel from Essex, view the place, and return all in a day, and as we returned, our thoughts were that there had been even more tall, dark trees, even more rooks, and that the house was even more gloomy than it is.'

In the 100 years following the church's consecration, Landscove's parishioners knew only five

Rhododendron yunnanense, a feature of the colourful border which separates the east side of the lawn from the Temple Garden and Rhododendron Walk.

A very large specimen of Rhamnus alaterna 'Argenteo-variegata', thought by some to be the most beautiful of variegated shrubs.

different incumbents. Villagers can recall a fine vicarage garden and still, today, the occasional past parishioner, returning to recapture childhood memories, is welcomed by Mr. Hubbard. But in 1958 the parish of Landscove was re-united with Staverton; the vicarage was put up for sale and its garden (by then something of a wilderness), submitted itself to the inspired hands of its first lay owner, the Renaissance figure of Edward Hyams.

Hyams had begun the war as an able seaman and risen to Commander by its close, having become an expert in the then novel science of radar. After the war he settled in Kent -'I liked Kent,' he wrote, 'it is near London but also near France and has the next best thing to a dry, continental climate one can find in Britain.' He became widely travelled, responding 'to the most pleasing objects of nature and art with a kind of delighted astonishment that such things should be.' Italy inspired his interest in the art of garden design, and his wife communicated to him her interest and pleasure in wild flowers. The two interests combined, and garden-making became his 'most sustained and sustaining pleasure'. In Kent he learned the science of plants and horticultural skills from people he met there, later confessing, 'I'm a very good brain-picker.' In truth, of the villagers at Landscove that remember him some recall 'a rather peculiar character, very conversational provided he was learning something from you, but once he had what he required he'd be off.' In Kent he had reintroduced the remontant strawberry to English horticulture and, alongside Mr. Ray Barrington-Brock in Surrey, had brought back viticulture to Britain. He had also become gardening correspondent for *The Illustrated London News* and had written novels, and three textbooks for amateurs on fruit-growing.

Hyams' approach was inter-disciplinary, for him art and science were never distinct. Allan Jackson, lecturer in horticulture at Wye College (the Agricultural and Horticultural College of London University) was chosen by Hyams as his gardening guru at that time because, 'he has the gift . . . of being able to relate [horticulture] to the other arts and sciences and to life in general.'

By 1960, Hyams had gathered a great deal of knowledge and was ready to practise gardening as an art. 'I believe that my whole attitude to the garden changed in a single day, the day, even before we moved into our new house [at Landscove], which I spent looking at the great garden at Dartington Hall.'

Today Hyams' garden is open to the public, and much remains of his original plan and planting. Unhappily, in 1968, his marriage came to an end and Hyams left Landscove. In financial straits, his wife sold many of the great rhododendrons to Dartington Hall, the fount of Hyams' original inspiration for the garden. But Landscove's present owner is gradually restoring all to his original specifications. The one big change does not really affect the garden plan at all because it is screened from the garden proper: Hyams had converted the most southerly acreage into a vineyard, but that has long since housed commercial greenhouses from which today Raymond Hubbard runs a prosperous and innovative nursery and plant centre.

The only change to Pearson's design of the outside of the house has been the Church Room, a building stuck onto the west of the house by one of the five ecclesiastic incumbents of Landscove. Hyams' reaction to the hideous addition was to remove its front and side walls, prop the roof up with wooden columns and beams and use it as a summer house, or as he called it a loggia. He laid the floor in Carrera marble, which his wife had picked up for a song at a fishmonger's that had closed down. 'Laying that marble floor was one of those tasks which become a sort of nagging obsession,' wrote Hyams. 'We put down a three-inch layer of sand and raked it level and it was then a matter of laying the three different colours in such a manner as to make a pleasing and symmetrical pattern . . .'

'The only trouble was that the three-inch layer of sand was laid on the wooden floor,' recalls Mr. Hubbard, 'and two years after he moved out, the floor collapsed!'

We have rebuilt the walls of the room, but you can still see his 'very distinguished, very distinct and tender Macartney rose' (*Rosa bracteata*), though it only just survived the hard winter of 1986. It is almost evergreen and later it has large single white cupped flowers with a yellow centre. Hyams noted that it is one of the easiest roses to propagate by cuttings.

The view of the Pearson church from the garden.

The loggia.

. . . in their young leaf the moutans are perhaps the most beautiful of all shrubs; not only are the finely lobed and divided leaves very pretty in form, but the soft coppery-reds, bronzed blue-greens, and pewter-greens, are among the most lovely colours in nature.'

On the front of the house grows *Lonicera x purpusii*, a creamy white, very fragrant flower that comes in time for Christmas and lasts until March. 'The west wall of the house is covered with slates,' explains Mr. Hubbard, 'because we get horizontal rain in these parts: it travels about a quarter of a mile across land before it hits the ground, and the west is the side most exposed to rain. At some point the slates on the south and east walls needed to be replaced but instead, the Church Commissioners – "notoriously sharp landlords" according to Hyams – used a concrete facing. So ugly did Hyams find this by comparison with the west side, that he planted *Parthenocissus henryana*, a fruitless vine that clings to the wall with suckers, has no flowers but leaves with a fantastic marbled effect all summer. He also put in variegated ivies and for the worst patches of concrete, *Pileostegia viburnoides*, which is related to the hydrangea and has the same sort of flowers.'

To complete a winter feast of flowering shrubs there is a *Clematis cirrhosa balearica*, out between January and March and a *Viburnum x bodnantense* 'which must be one of the longest flowering shrubs of all,' Mr. Hubbard points out, 'normally about eight months' flowering and over the winter period.

'Edward Hyams was very fond of myrtles and quite a few remain – *Myrtus communis tarentina* and *M. luma*, and we have added *M. ugni*. A tarentina provides the classical link to his Temple Garden – "[The Tarentina] is an ancient plant," he wrote, "for according to Bean, 'Recognisable twigs have been

Besides the Macartney, his *Rosa banksiae* 'Lutea' (the double yellow Banksian rose) survives, as does a *montana* clematis and one of his vines. The choisya was Hyams', as were the summer flowering jasmine and his passion, geraniums: 'I have a taste for the genus,' he wrote, 'and in my opinion the finest species of them all is the native Great Meadow Cranesbill, *Geranium pratense*. It is a curious thing that this limestone plant grows with terrific vigour in our garden – where, after all, many species of rhododendron flourish . . . Its foliage is extremely handsome and the large blue flowers much finer than those of the exotics. Another native limestone geranium is very much at home with us, the "Bloody Cranesbill".'

On the south wall of the house grow his wistaria and a chaenomeles, the variety 'Knap Hill Scarlet', the only plant on the walls that Hyams inherited. Also on the south border one paeony survives, *P. lutea*, though Hyams recalls 'we planted a number of moutans, one of them being the type *P. suffruticosa*

171

On the house wall, Wistaria, Rosa 'Banksiae' and Chaenomeles 'Knap Hill Scarlet'. The centre shrub, Paeonia ludlowii, dominates a border which also includes delphiniums, several roses and Ceratostigma willmottianum.

Choisya ternata.

found in Roman tombs of 2,000 years ago.' Its leaves are miniature, its stature dwarf, its shape symmetrical and it flowers freely." The Temple Garden was planted in the broken shade of two big pittosporum trees, so big in fact that they formed the substance of an article by him in *The Royal Horticultural Society* magazine. These have now gone but I am pleased to say that we have a seedling here which we hope will do just as well.'

To complete the classical theme Hyams planted 'six bushes of that deciduous azalea native to Asia Minor (not too remote from the Hellenic theme) whose honey poisoned so many of Xenophon's Ten Thousand on their march to the sea, as told in the *Anabasis*. The plant was formerly called *Azalea pontica* but is now called *Rhododendron luteum*.'

The temple itself was bought from 'an antique shop . . . too superior to be called a junk-shop'. Close to, it has the insubstantial feel of an actor's prop but

succeeds in its function. 'The idea was to sit up at the temple, look down through the azaleas along what he called, rather grandly, the rhododendron walk,' explains Mr. Hubbard. Hyams felled two large yews to make way for the walk but was forbidden by his wife 'who fights for the life of every tree I want to remove' from felling more. In the darkest part by what he called Rond Point, commanded by an enormous Scots pine, he planted the European *Rhododendron ponticeum*, which managed to flower in almost total absence of light, and, 'by way of a change', *R. maximum*, its North American equivalent. Emerging from Rond Point he had a pair of *R. calophytum*, but the majority of rhododendrons composing the vista were of the *grande* series 'and should, long after I am dead, give distinction to this garden and cause me to be blessed for planting a kind of rhododendrons which, because they do not flower in youth, is too rarely planted by modern gardeners.'

Unfortunately, as already mentioned, this was not to be, though quite a few can still be seen in Dartington Hall gardens. 'We want to put some of them back again,' Mr. Hubbard says. 'Of the *grande* series we have planted *R. macabeanum*, probably the finest for garden purposes of the large-leaved rhododendrons and among the hardiest of the series. I am pleased to see that it has emerged from last winter unscathed and is growing like mad. But we will not have as many, preferring to keep the walk more as a natural woodland setting.'

The other main feature of the garden, which remains completely unaltered since Hyams' day is the water garden and greenhouse. 'This he really did well,' says Mr. Hubbard. 'The water always stays clear; people ask me the secret which must be that it has the right balance of plants and animal life.' The

Rond Point, off which Hyams' Rhododendron Walk led, is commanded by an enormous Scots pine.

Right. The Temple Garden beyond the well-scented Rhododendron luteum.
Below. Looking from Rond Point past Rhododendron ponticum, down the Rhododendron Walk.

Edward Hyams' water garden. In the foreground, Welsh poppies (Meconopsis cambrica), on the far side kingcups, white and pink water lilies, around the path are scented pinks, lemon scented verbena, blue Convolvulus sabaticus, pink C. althaeoides, chocolate-scented Cosmos atrosanguineus, and the prostrate Malvastrum lateritium which has brick-red flowers.

greenhouse retains his seven vines, all of the variety 'Muscat of Alexandra', grown from cuttings which he brought from Kent. There are peaches, 'Amsden June' and a nectarine, and a 'Meyer's Lemon' – 'Having grown, in my time, all the hardy fruits and some of the less hardy ones, I can say that I have never grown any that gave less trouble than lemons,' Hyams declared and Mr. Hubbard can only agree: 'Some years we have had sixty lemons – commercial size – from his planting.'

Rhododendron 'Irene Koster' backed by Hyams' bamboos. In spring this area is a carpet of snowdrops and primroses.

Other Gardens to Visit

The Old Parsonage at Sutton Valence in Kent (left), was built in 1720. A steeply sloping garden has been terraced and planted with trees, shrubs, roses, ground coverers, and mixed herbaceous plants. There is a *Rosa* 'Wolley Dod' commemorating the Reverend Charles Wolley Dod, to whose nineteenth-century cultivations the fine modern development of our Michaelmas daisies owes a great debt. The picture looks past an ancient nut planting towards the ruins of Sutton Valence Castle, which is part of the parsonage garden and will be open to the public from 1988. *Contact*: Mrs. R. Perks.

The garden at the famous Parsonage at Haworth in Yorkshire (bottom left), is under expert restoration by Mr. P.R. Swindells of Harlow Car Gardens ('the Wisley of the North'). The plan has been to include plants that belong to the era during which the Brontë family lived here. Tangled informality was the order of the day and decorative, herbal and economic plants were all grown in close proximity. The picture shows the two firs planted by the Brontës, between which the sisters' coffins were carried to church and final resting place. *Contact*: Mrs. M. Raistrick, Custodian.

The Old Vicarage, Church Stretton in Shropshire was built about 1815. A new garden, planted for minimum maintenance and to integrate the splendid surrounding views, has evolved since 1970 when today's owner, Mr. W.B. Hutchinson took it over. He has concentrated on ornamental trees, flowering shrubs, roses, primulas, and irises in the newly renovated water garden.

Vicar's Mead, East Budleigh in Devon, was built in 1484-5 and is redolent of historical intrigue. Sir Walter Raleigh, whose birthplace is nearby, had his early schooling here, and in the eighteenth century it was the headquarters of a large smuggling organisation. The 'smuggling vicars', Matthew Munday (1741) and Ambrose Stapleton (1794) operated from here. The present owners, Mr. and Mrs. H.F.J. Read have made a fascinating and unusual garden out of its three and a half acres, which includes more than 4,500 plants. There are sixty varieties alone in the hosta garden, part of which is shown here (top right), and there are four National Collections of rare plants.

The Old Rectory, Farnborough in Berkshire (bottom left), built in 1749, was bought by John Betjeman during the war. Beautiful views and herbacious plantings, and a recently planted woodland water garden. See also the John Piper window in Betjeman's memory in the church across the road. *Contact*: Mrs. M. Todhunter.

The Old Palace of Southwell, Nottinghamshire (far right). A Palace of the Archbishops of York has stood here since the foundation of the Minster in 956. Centuries later it was the home of Cardinal Wolsey. Finally, it was laid to ruin by the Cromwellians. The ruins are now a feature of the garden and include plantings on religious themes within their walls. *Contact*: The Bishop's Private Secretary.

The National Gardens Scheme
A complete list of private gardens open to the public may be purchased from The NGS Charitable Trust, 57 Lower Belgrave Street, London, SW1.